PRAISE FOR *THE YES E*

Luis Bush is a global visionary who carries the heartbeat of God to bring hope and transformational change to the poor, oppressed, and downtrodden of the world through the message of salvation and the principles of God's word. I highly encourage you to discover his secrets through reading The Yes Effect. They will work, whether the next step God is asking you to take is big or small.

Loren Cunningham | Founder of Youth With a Mission (YWAM)

If the immensity of the world's suffering makes you feel powerless, *The Yes Effect* is assigned reading. Its stories of real people saying yes to God illustrate the urgent task of loving God by loving God's world. This book compels us to see those who suffer and to weep with them. It also invites us to pray and to work for the kingdom coming on earth as it is in heaven.

Jen Pollock Michel | Author of *Teach Us to Want* and *Keeping Place*

Luis Bush is a leader who embodies the gospel as well as anyone I know. If you are serious about making an impact on this world for the cause of Christ, Luis has always had much to say worth pondering. Listen to him and be moved!

Barry H. Corey | President of Biola University and author of *Love Kindness*

We are so thankful for Luis and Doris Bush's vision and passion—to reach the most needy, lost, and broken people of the world. May these inspiring stories move the hearts of many to say yes to the Lord's call in their lives and to bring the gospel, wherever God leads, to the ends of the earth.

Lane and Ebeth Dennis | President and Executive Vice President of Publishing Ministry at Crossway

Luis Bush has been a magnificent example of helping to transform the world wherever he has gone. *The Yes Effect* is packed with stories of humble people who have transformed their cities by saying yes to God's invitation to change the world around us.

Paul Eshleman | Vice President of Campus Crusade for Christ International

Missionary tales were favorites of mine when I was young, but I stopped reading them as I grew up and sensed God calling me to put down roots and serve my neighbors. Reading this astonishing and beautiful testimony of God's work in the world, I saw with new eyes the value of my own small yes. When we say yes to God, even in small things, our hearts and then our communities can be transformed to an extent we might never have imagined. *The Yes Effect* revealed my own place in a much larger story of God's goodness and faithfulness and inspired me to go on, every day, saying yes.

Christie Purifoy | Blogger and author of *Roots and Sky*

A terrific book! From beginning to end, Luis graciously proclaims the love of God and salvation through faith in Jesus Christ while at the same time tirelessly reminding us of the pain and suffering of mankind. To such a world of need and desperation, the book gives a passionate call for Christians to step up and be enlisted in God's service to fulfill Christ's Great Commission by carrying on the task of reaching the world with the gospel!

Thomas Wang | Director of the first Chinese Congress on World Evangelization and President Emeritus of Great Commission Center International

Almost every dedicated Christian is aware of the "10/40 Window" but few know the origin of this unique focus on a swath of land stretching from southern Europe and North Africa to the Far East. Luis Bush shares the secret of a productive life for Christ: a sincere yes to anything God asks. I have witnessed the "yes effect" in the life of the author from his days as a student at Dallas Theological Seminary to his present amazing leadership in mission outreach all over the world. You will not want to miss reading this life-changing book.

J. Ronald Blue | Adjunct Professor in World Missions and Intercultural Studies at Dallas Theological Seminary

I had the privilege of serving as Luis Bush's pastor in the early 90s. He soon became my mentor, birthing and shaping in me a passion for world missions that changed the trajectory of my ministry. If you know Luis, you know him as a visionary who can coalesce leaders from across the globe like none other. If you don't know Luis, read *The Yes Effect* for the compelling stories and contagious passion. You might just put it down to go out and change your world.

Daniel Henderson | President of Strategic Renewal and Author of *Old Paths, New Power*

Luis Bush, an experienced leader, gives us excellent advice in this book. Because we know that God gives the gifts of the Holy Spirit to every believer, and that each of us is unique in our gifts and context, he encourages us to use those gifts by listening for and responding to God with a resounding yes! When you do, amazing things will happen.

Paul E. Pierson | Dean Emeritus and Senior Professor of History of Mission and Latin American Studies at Fuller Theological Seminary

It's easy to look at all the needs in the world, the extreme brokenness and lostness, and to feel overwhelmed. But you will be encouraged, strengthened, and inspired as you read *The Yes Effect*. You couldn't have a better guide weaving together stories of how the Lord has shown up again and again and helping you move from despair to glad engagement.

Michael Young-Suk Oh | Global Executive Director/CEO of the Lausanne Movement

In a culture increasingly shouting no to the beauty of the calling of Jesus Christ, Luis Bush gives his readers every reason to shout yes to the mission of the gospel. Whether you share the power of the cross with the local bank teller or an unreached tribe, as Luis says, "We take on God's heart when we refuse to look away."

Denise Jones | Author of *Reclaiming Your Heart* | Founder and President of Reclaiming Hearts Ministries

In our ministry, we often talk about the immeasurable effect of "small" and simple acts of ministry. When I think of the power of yes, I think of Luis Bush. He has truly revolutionized much of the way the church thinks and approaches world evangelization. Through moving stories and deeply rooted hope, *The Yes Effect* leads us on a journey to engaging the real (and sometimes overwhelming) need in our world through the compassionate heart of God, uncovering how each of us can boldly and practically say yes to God right where we are. Begin your "yes effect" journey by saying yes to reading this book.

Dick Eastman | International President of Every Home for Christ

Jesus commanded His followers to disciple the nations first by the transformation of individual lives through salvation and then through them to transform the lives, structures, and cultures around them. Luis Bush invites our participation by drawing on his own unusual life and ministries and upon those men and women of the global networks he has nurtured. These pages contain many inspiring stories of how ordinary people have been used by God to do extraordinary things in today's world. May you also be inspired to obey God's call!

Patrick Johnstone | Author Emeritus at Operation World

The Yes Effect is gripping and beautifully written. I could not put it down! Each chapter is filled with captivating stories that illustrate a greater challenge for each of us. I recommend it to anyone who isn't afraid to have their heart stirred.

Kristin Berry | Author of *Born Broken: An Adoptive Journey*

Luis Bush and his wife, Doris, have been calling the international church to get knee-deep in transformational ministry for many years. What this means is seen here in the lives of real people who in different situations have moved out with God to change their world. *The Yes Effect* shows us that it is as inspiring as it is challenging to go into action where we are planted.

Robert E. Coleman | Speaker, professor, and author of *The Master Plan of Evangelism*

Do you want to know what it means to say yes to God? After the Bible itself, your wisest counsel is likely to come from someone like Luis Bush, one of our generation's global church leaders. *The Yes Effect* is chock-full of hard-won wisdom and is highly recommended for every Christian who aspires to a life of useful obedience.

Duane Litfin | Former President of Wheaton College (1993–2010)

THE
YES
EFFECT

Accepting God's Invitation to Transform the World Around You

LUIS BUSH

with Darcy Wiley

MOODY PUBLISHERS

CHICAGO

Unless otherwise indicated, Scripture quotations are from the ESV® Bible (The Holy Bible, English Standard Version®), copyright © 2001 by Crossway, a publishing ministry of Good News Publishers. Used by permission. All rights reserved.

Scripture quotations marked NIV are taken from the Holy Bible, New International Version®, NIV®, Copyright © 1973, 1978, 1984, 2011 by Biblica, Inc.™ Used by permission of Zondervan. All rights reserved worldwide. www.zondervan.com The "NIV" and "New International Version" are trademarks registered in the United States Patent and Trademark Office by Biblica, Inc.™

Scripture quotations marked AMPC are taken from the Amplified Bible, Copyright © 1954, 1958, 1962, 1964, 1965, 1987 by The Lockman Foundation. Used by permission.

Scripture quotations marked The Message are taken from *The Message*, copyright © 1993, 1994, 1995, 1996, 2000, 2001, 2002 by Eugene H. Peterson. Used by permission of NavPress. All rights reserved. Represented by Tyndale House Publishers, Inc.

Published in association with The Craig Wiley Agency.

Edited by Kevin P. Emmert
Interior and cover design: Erik M. Peterson
Cover art of push pins and thread copyright © 2017 by pogonici / Shutterstock (168037637). All rights reserved.

Library of Congress Cataloging-in-Publication Data

Names: Bush, Luis, author.
Title: The yes effect : accepting God's invitation to transform the world around you / Luis Bush with Darcy Wiley.
Description: Chicago : Moody Publishers, 2017. | Includes bibliographical references.
Identifiers: LCCN 2017024071 (print) | LCCN 2017032655 (ebook) | ISBN 9780802495822 | ISBN 9780802415936
Subjects: LCSH: Missions. | Missionary stories.
Classification: LCC BV2063 (ebook) | LCC BV2063 .B866 2017 (print) | DDC 266--dc23
LC record available at https://lccn.loc.gov/2017024071

We hope you enjoy this book from Moody Publishers. Our goal is to provide high-quality, thought-provoking books and products that connect truth to your real needs and challenges. For more information on other books and products written and produced from a biblical perspective, go to www.moodypublishers.com or write to:

Moody Publishers
820 N. LaSalle Boulevard
Chicago, IL 60610

1 3 5 7 9 10 8 6 4 2

Printed in the United States of America

To Jesus, the author and finisher of my faith.
Thank You for giving Your life that I may
live mine to the fullest.

Contents

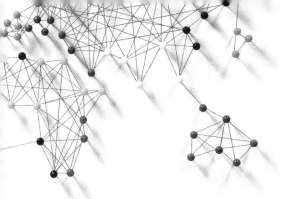

Foreword

As you picked up this book, you took the first step on a very rewarding pilgrimage. Maybe that was decision number 999 you made today. Thousands of times a day, we stand at the crossroads of saying yes or no to choices that come before us—click here, buy this, support that. We're hyper-stressed from over-packed lives that cry out for us to stand ever vigilant deciding what and how much we can say yes to and still maintain a balanced and purposeful life.

In reading Luis Bush's *The Yes Effect*, you will take a joyful journey into the lives of amazing people across the globe who have realized their potential and God's will by saying yes to the right things at the right time for the right reasons. For some, the yes decision means simply their quiet, timely blessing of one other person who desperately needed their hug, prayer, encouragement, or rescue. For others, their yes moment has led to transformed communities—even nations. As you'll soon read, a thoughtful, prayerful, and obedient yes leads to an adventurous, faith-stretching odyssey that culminates in joy. The world is blessed and the kingdom of God expands as faithful people say yes to those whispered invitations from God that may seem uncomfortable, impossible, illogical, too sacrificial, or even dangerous.

A fearful or stubborn no to God leads to "what if," "if only," and "shoulda, coulda, woulda" regrets. But it's our choice to make. The great tragedy of saying no to God is that we'll never experience the unsurpassed joy of a divinely orchestrated achievement that could have been life-changing not only for us, but also for those He intended to bless through us, including those in following generations.

Personally, I am deeply indebted to a powerful yes decision made by a young couple during World War II. Childhood sweethearts, Ken and Marge grew up in a very missions-minded church in Denver and listened to many visiting missionaries from around the world. The tales from Africa—accompanied by show-and-tell python skins and scorpions in jars—always seemed to be the scariest. They prayed that youthful prayer: "Lord, please don't call me to be a missionary. But if You do, please—not to Africa!"

Ken was drafted into the Navy, and Marge, then his fiancée, went off to Moody Bible Institute in Chicago to study while he was gone. They were madly in love and had a life plan, which definitely did not involve missions. But during shore leave, on a rickshaw ride through China's crowded streets, Ken suddenly sensed from the Lord, "Ken, I want you to be a fisher of men." The call was so clear that when he got back to his ship, he sat on his bunk and with a broken heart wrote to his sweetheart: "Marge, today in China, God unmistakably called me to be a missionary. I am so sorry, I know this means the end of our life together, but I must say yes. I must obey my Lord." He could have affixed the stamp with his tears.

Meanwhile, that same day in Chicago, at a missions conference at Moody, Marge received the same message. On her dorm room bed she wrote to her beloved Ken, "I must obey, I must say yes. I am so very sorry." And you probably guessed it—their letters crossed in the mail between China and Chicago. God has a great sense of humor—Ken and Marge not only served as missionaries for thirty-five years, but spent many of those years in Africa!

Ken and Marge, now with the Lord, are my parents, and I lived my childhood among the poor of a West African village. Long story short: my heart, soul, and character were shaped by that loving community, which led me to 40 years of service to children and the poor with the ministry of Compassion International. I owe it all to a young couple's yes to God.

By saying yes to God, we join the long procession of those who have gone before us, not only our parents and grandparents, but all the way back to those brothers and sisters in faith from the early church. Their yes to God created the opportunity for us to take our place in the great chain reaction that will live long beyond us as still others say yes and pick up where we left off. As Luis says, one small yes after another has changed the course of history.

Knowing Luis as the mastermind of the 10/40 Window missions strategy, I have been fascinated to discover his own story as, yes by yes, he has introduced the oppressed and hopeless to a life-giving relationship with Jesus. Our paths crossed when Luis researched the 4/14 Window, which is a demographic window representing children ages four to fourteen, the most undervalued and unreached of all.

Luis's passion ignited as his research revealed people in that age group to be the most receptive to the gospel. Sadly, this group was also historically the forgotten "least of these." As Luis points out, missions and churches devote less than three percent of their resources toward reaching and discipling them. Thankfully, Luis said yes to the challenge, and the 4/14 Movement was launched. As a fellow advocate for these little ones, I shudder to think what would have happened—or more tragically, wouldn't have happened—if Luis and his wife, Doris, had stood at that crossroads and not said yes.

In *The Yes Effect*, Luis tells tale after tale of people he has known from his lifetime of world travels who have come to that crossroads and said yes. Some faced great danger, some confronted impossible odds, some had enormous vision only God could have planted and then brought to fruition. After reading some stories, I put the book down and, inspired, thought, Hey, I could do that! After other stories, I bowed my head, fought back tears and thought, If only I had that kind of courage and faith!

As Luis says, "Just because your story doesn't appear in this book doesn't mean God isn't writing it." I believe in the power of saying yes to God's invitations in our unique places and pursuits. I believe in listening for opportunities to say yes. I believe in being open to the adventures God has planned for us. By the end of this book, I know you will too.

WESS STAFFORD
President Emeritus, Compassion International

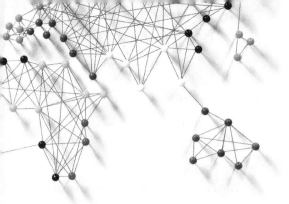

Follow Your Leaders

I leaned toward the nearly invisible layer protecting me from the free fall that waited just on the other side. Many years earlier, brave workers had secured lengths of steel rebar, concrete, and sturdy glass to construct this building in place of dilapidated tenement homes. There in our friends' high-rise apartment, we met with a half-dozen young couples for our weekly Bible study. Up in the air, our feet were on solid ground. From that vantage point, I stood at ease, looking down at the tiny people buzzing about in the city's streets. The myriad elements of the urban scene displayed themselves like a miniature model of a city.

Below us, the grid of Chicago, in 1972, stretched along the lakeshore with other high-rises in view. Just south from there, the new John Hancock skyscraper reached skyward and the even newer Sears Tower, still under construction at the time, rose up to take its place as the tallest building in the world. In that section of the city, the Chicago River cut through the geometric lines of gray streets, squares of grass, blocks of townhouses, factories, shops, and apartment buildings. Once upon a time, the river had flowed in the opposite direction. It wasn't until civil engineers in the late 1800s reversed its natural flow, coaxing water from Lake Michigan to increase the city's water supply, that the river took its modern form.[1]

From our perch, we could see the "L" train lines hovering over old alleys, taking fellow Chicagoans home from construction sites, offices, and schools. Before the modern routes had been constructed, public transportation existed as a mere scattering of rail lines working as separate entities, controlled by separate companies.[2] Much had changed in that city over the decades, and we were beneficiaries of it.

Fresh out of college with an economics degree, and married to the love of my life, Doris, I spent my days in the heart of Chicago doing system design and computer programming work in the management services department of the Arthur Andersen headquarters, one of the Big Five accounting firms of the era. My dad had always taught me to invest in learning and using the latest technology and innovations. It would open all kinds of doors for me, he assured. Now, heeding his advice, I was working for this prestigious company and making a life in one of the largest cities in the United States.

Born a citizen of Argentina to parents of British descent, I grew up speaking three languages and bouncing between hometowns. I spent much of my youth in Brazil, went back to do military service in Argentina, and studied at the University of North Carolina. I felt like I was from everywhere and nowhere all at the same time. But there in the grid of Chicago, I was starting to find my place.

Some of our friends were moving into houses and laying

foundations for a long future in the Windy City. Doris and I were prepared to do the same, saving up for a down payment on a condo. But there in our friends' high-rise apartment as we studied the Bible with other young businesspeople, God was giving Doris and me a bird's eye view not only of the city, but of His kingdom, too.

As we gathered in that living room above all the hustle and bustle below, He began to reveal the grandness of His kingdom's infrastructure and His long-term plan for it. Soon we sensed Him inviting us to become personally involved in the continued expansion of that beneficent kingdom here on earth. We could not remain as spectators looking on. He wanted us to go beyond reading the blueprint in the pages of the Bible to become living, breathing kingdom builders involved directly in the growth of the worldwide community of Christ. Believers can do that in Chicago, to be sure. In fact, today Doris and I call Chicago home once again, a landing pad that allows us to be close to our family. Thanks to the international airports in the area, we are "close" to the rest of the world, too. We get to watch our grandchildren grow while still encouraging the growth of the church around the globe. But back in our early adulthood, though we had been excited about putting down roots and settling into the American dream in our adopted city, we were starting to sense that God might be asking us to hold our residency in Chicago loosely, to be untethered and ready to move, not knowing that He would one day bring us back.

The night before we were to sign the papers for the condo, as we gathered in prayer with our brothers and sisters there in that skyscraper apartment, we knew God was telling us to forfeit the opportunity we so wanted to seize. Though we were to remain in Chicago for a time, it became clear that He didn't want us to plant our roots there yet. The next day, we told our realtor that we wouldn't be moving in. And we began waiting to see how God was going to move from there.

When I joined the consultancy division of Arthur Andersen, my supervisors presented their plans to make me manager in Brazil after six years at the international office in Chicago. It was an attractive offer that would grow my career, use my skills in strategy and administration, and put me back in São Paulo, Brazil, the place where my parents and brothers still lived. It sounded like the perfect fit, so I accepted. Yet as Doris and I went to visit Brazil and prepare for the move back to our home continent, we began to see more than just a business need in that part of the world. We also sensed a spiritual need, and along with it, a call from the Lord to return to Latin America and invest our time and energy in a whole different way than the one we had expected. We knew we could serve the Lord in either capacity, whether in business or full-time ministry, and we knew there was a real need for His people to do both, but we couldn't shake the feeling that God was specifically and personally inviting Doris and me to a new task in our old familiar territory.

DRAWN TO THE LIGHT

Visiting my childhood city, I thought back on my reputation during my early years and reflected on the ways I had changed since coming to know the Lord. I hadn't always been known to say yes to the best things. As a youth, I had put my energy toward pursuits that impacted our community in a not-so-positive way. As a ten-year-old in Brazil, I rounded up my peers in the São Paulo neighborhood where we lived and held a secret meeting one night at an empty house owned by my family. If my friends wanted to be part of the neighborhood gang, I told them, they had to do one mischievous deed each day. I held up the list by candlelight for them to study. Then, we went out to the streets.

We rang doorbells and ran away before the homeowner could get to the door. We let the air out of our neighbors' car tires. And we did some other things, too, but I'll plead the fifth on all that. It didn't take long for us to build a bad reputation in the aftermath of our escapades. Before I knew it, the law caught up with me, and one evening an officer stepped onto my porch to ring my doorbell. Unlike us hoodlums, this officer apparently didn't think it would be humorous to ring our doorbell and run. He stood stoic and unyielding when my father opened the door.

I couldn't run, not this time. So I did the only thing I could. I hid. I slid behind the front door as the officer gave my father the lowdown on all the vandalism happening in the neighborhood. "We've heard the ringleader lives at this address," the officer said. I knew he wasn't there to compliment my leadership skills. And this was no prank. This was it. I was caught.

I remember that moment in utter clarity, how I peeked through the crack and braced myself for the moment that the door would close and I'd be left to deal with my father's discipline. Let's just say that night brought about a swift and permanent end to my neighborhood troublemaking. While the punishment wasn't pleasant, I'm grateful for my father's firm guidance and enduring concern for my lifelong well-being. This ringleader had a great leader to follow.

Although there was a change in my behavior that night, it wasn't until much later, on a trip back to Argentina in my college years, that my real transformation began. I had just finished my first two years of general courses as I worked toward my economics degree at UNC. At that time, I returned to Argentina for mandatory military service. A break from my studies didn't seem like such a bad idea. I had been lucky to be accepted into UNC in the first place and had been a mediocre student to prove it. I seemed to excel much more on the rugby field than I did in the classroom. After two years of struggling to keep a C average, I needed a change of pace. I just didn't know how much of a change I was walking, or marching, into.

When I arrived at boot camp in Argentina, I heard the shouts of officers giving commands to new recruits as they did push-ups. I gave my name to the military officer at the registration desk. "Bush," I said, watching the officer's pen attack the paper.

"Puff," he wrote.

"B-U-S-H," I corrected, with some level of confidence.

"It doesn't matter what your name is here," the officer shot back at me. And just like that, whatever confidence I had was gone. I scooted along with my head down, doing my duty, feeling my inferiority and invisibility from that moment on. But in that kind of environment, invisibility isn't always a bad thing.

They gave me a bent-up tin soup plate and gaucho pants that were several sizes too big, and each mealtime we would sit back to back on the dirty ground and eat the same bland mash. Finally, the day came when we could see visitors. My Grandma

Phyllis showed up without warning and brought me a container of roasted chicken. This was gold. I immediately crept to my tent and placed the contraband delicacy between my pillow and the straw mattress. But as soon as the visitors left, one officer called us to attention while the other inspected the tents. He pulled out that roasted chicken and promptly signed me up for two weeks of cleaning duties to pay for my offense.

Military service was starting to feel like prison. But one evening, when camp life had me hanging my head, something forced me to look up. It was my turn for watch duty. As I stood at my post somewhat dazed and daydreaming about going back to UNC, another officer, a committed Roman Catholic, approached me.

"Hey," he said, pointing up as if he were shooting a gun into the sky. I tilted my head, half expecting to see smoke rising from his fingertip. But there was no smoke. The sky was perfectly clear. The stars burned bright.

"How do you think those stars got there?" the officer asked.

Whether I was shy or felt better remaining unnoticed, I kept quiet.

"God made those, you know," he went on.

"Nah," I said under my breath.

He brushed his hand over his uniform and scoffed, unimpressed by my response, unimpressed by anything about me.

"You've got all this education and still you don't know who made those lights to guard the night?"

My eyes rolled a bit before looking up again. This time, though, my eyes went in and out of focus with the magnitude and depth of the dome of stars above me. The scene was now over my head in every way. Then my mind's eye took over, thinking on the shape of the constellations. I began connecting the dots of Centaurus and Musca. Between them was Crux, the shape of the cross. It wouldn't be the last time that shape would meet my eyes.

Not long after that jarring encounter with the officer and the stars above, I was reassigned to serve in Buenos Aires. It was a welcome assignment as the Keetons, my girlfriend Doris's family, lived in the area. On Easter Sunday, my grandmother and I were invited to lunch at their place. Gran saw me getting a little boisterous and hinted that I should settle down and change my behavior on account of the special occasion and the young lady at the table. Behave. That message was coming at me from all sides.

A few days later, after traveling to visit my family in São Paulo, Brazil, Crux confronted me again. This time, it showed up in the dotted constellation design on the Brazilian flag. Next, it showed up in the cross emblazoned on the Bible my brother John carried around. He had just returned from a silent retreat at Cambridge, where he had read Erasmus's *Letters to the Pope* and Augustine's *Confessions*. He couldn't stop speaking of what he'd learned.

When Doris came to visit from Argentina, we followed my brother's trend and began to read together. First, we read some of the classic writings my brother suggested. Then we opened Scripture itself. Soon our curiosity couldn't contain itself. We found ourselves accompanying my brother to church, to a local Protestant chapel.

On our first visit, the pastor read from Revelation about a world of famine, war, and disease, and about a Savior who will someday return to set it all right. We were captivated. We had never viewed the world through this lens, and we began to search Scripture for ourselves, exploring the redeeming work and coming return of Christ. We were compelled to keep digging deeper, planting ourselves in the rich soil of God's Word. One day, as Doris and I met with the pastor of the little chapel, he opened the Bible to another part of Revelation—the passage where Jesus pursues a people who have gone cold in their love for Him.

"I stand at the door and knock," Jesus says, urging apathetic believers to renew their love. "If anyone hears my voice and opens the door, I will come in" (Rev. 3:20). Though originally crafted for a church in need of fresh communion with Jesus, that message spoke to me that day, to someone who was just getting to know Him. It was the hour, *my* hour, to accept Jesus' offer. He wanted me to open the door, not to crouch behind it and peer through the crack, trembling in fear of judgment. This time I stood at the threshold to welcome Jesus in, knowing only He could remake this mischief-maker, this mediocre student, this lackluster soldier. Only He could save me.

When Jesus comes in, He shakes things up. He changes His followers in heart, soul, and mind. To me, the flailing student, He gave clarity and motivation. I directed my new energy toward finishing my economics degree at UNC. At that same time, Doris felt the call to extend the invitation of Jesus to her family and friends in Argentina. Our faith would grow over the next two years in our separate lives as I finished school and Doris stayed in South America. When the time was right, we threw in our lot together in a shared life of faith as Doris flew up from warm Argentina to marry me in Chicago on the coldest day of 1971.

A PATH REVEALED

Now, ready to put down roots in Chicago, we were being presented with our first big choice as a married couple. We were going back to Latin America. That much was clear. But would I be investing myself in Arthur Andersen there as a business consultant or would I be accepting this unexpected invitation to serve the Lord in a different way, stepping out from the work I was used to? Early on in our marriage, Doris and I had dealt with minor disagreements, as all couples do. But in this area, we were totally aligned. With confidence, I resigned and closed the book on my promising career in Chicago.

This is not to say that all believers should leave the business world to take on full-time vocational ministry. I share this story with you as a description of what God did in my situation, not as a prescription for what should happen in yours. Some might be called specifically to engage in the business world. Others might clearly be called to full-time vocational ministry, like Doris and I were. Others still might be given the invitation to choose between the two—with neither path being the wrong way to go—or even to do both at the same time in something we call "business as mission." Most often, though, following Jesus in our daily lives looks like weaving our mission in with our skilled trades, office jobs, and home life. Each of us receives our own invitations to work and serve in our unique contexts, and these various avenues for engaging our talents, skills, and passions all contribute to vibrant societies and a growing local church.

God's invitations are particular and personal, but not always predictable. Sometimes we get a birds-eye view; other times we can see nothing but the step in front of us. After all, we serve a God who called Abraham to go without knowing where God was leading him, a God who led His people forty years through the wilderness to a land they'd never seen. His instructions come according to His vision and His timing, and in our case, that involved a time of preparation before moving back to South America. Though I had recently finished my undergrad, we sensed God wanted me to go right back to school, to attend Dallas Theological Seminary in preparation for the work awaiting us in Latin America. I spent the next four and a half years working on my master's while simultaneously working the night shift at a local business and pastoring a small Spanish-speaking church in West Dallas. It was an exciting time of learning.

Although we knew we were heading to Latin America after I graduated, we had no idea exactly where we'd be going. We prayed and waited with expectation. With increased knowledge and daily experience of the Lord's guidance and provision, our faith was growing stronger. There was no indication regarding what specific steps we were to take beyond seminary, so we just kept praying. We prayed and we waited all the way up to graduation day.

On graduation day of all days, we opened a letter asking us to serve at a church in El Salvador. But then things got interesting. We received another invitation to serve at the church in São Paulo, the very place where our pastor friend had led us to Christ years earlier. God had presented us with yet another choice to make.

I didn't sleep much that night. I tossed and turned under

the covers as I wrestled with God, and finally fell asleep for a short time. But when my bleary eyes awoke to His morning mercies, I had an undeniable sense that He was leading us to a place where we didn't have roots. He was leading us out of our comfort zone, away from the place we would naturally want to go. But it was more than that. I didn't have a list of reasons why, but I had a strong sense of knowing that God wasn't just leading us away from something; He was leading us *to* El Salvador. He was girding us up for adventure, strengthening our spiritual muscles by taking us to an unfamiliar place. It was a capacity we'd need for the larger work God would have in store for us further down the road.

KINGDOM BUILDERS

When we reported for duty at Iglesia Nazaret in El Salvador, we quickly realized that God wasn't just moving in us and moving us physically to a new place. He wasn't just moving in the church in El Salvador, either. We could tell right away that He was moving in the hearts of thousands of Latin Americans, even moving them physically to other places of gospel poverty. We kept hearing the loud whispers of a growing and unlikely passion: South America, where so many missionaries had been sent, was soon to become a missions-sending continent itself.

I began to sense this is why we had come. I immediately began exploring this momentum in the church. Working with a group called Partners International in Latin America, I led an inquiry to explore and discern the movement of the Holy Spirit on the continent, going to every country in Latin America to hear from the leadership of many different denominations.

Almost everywhere we visited, we found the believers of Latin America ready to go into all the earth to preach the gospel.

Soon, three thousand people convened in Brazil to launch a global missions movement from Latin America. A few years later, after staying put and enduring the horrific civil war in El Salvador, Doris and I got a new invitation. In order to enter more fully into research and inquiry, the new type of work God was preparing for me, I accepted the role of president of Partners International and prepared for a move back to the United States. Born in Argentina, raised in Brazil, and serving in El Salvador, I felt the same passion burning in me that was burning in the rest of my missions-minded brothers and sisters on the continent. In a way, I was being sent as one of the first representatives from Latin America to give voice to our vision inside the world of Christian missions strategy. So it was back to the States to work at the Partners International headquarters to increase the momentum for a new Latin American wave of missions.

The missions world as a whole could feel the rumbling, and when God shakes things up, it's tough for His people to ignore. Immediately following the Congress of Ibero American Missions, better known as COMIBAM '87, leadership from the well-known Lausanne Movement contacted me. The small gathering of Lausanne leaders, led by Dr. Thomas Wang, the International Director of Lausanne at that time, embraced the distinct call to connect influencers and ideas for global missions. They invited me to share the principles in the Latin American missions mobilization that led to COMIBAM '87, as well as what that might mean for the rest of the world as we looked to the year 2000.

After much research on the challenge before us, I presented my findings at their second global conference, Lausanne II, held in Manila, Philippines, in 1989. There we focused on the area of the world with the greatest human need and the greatest spiritual need. In my preparation, I lingered over the research of many past workers, thinkers, and writers whom God had used to pave the way in the study of missions. In the early 1900s, Samuel M. Zwemer's book *The Unoccupied Mission Fields of Africa and Asia* featured a map of the world highlighting countries without any Christian missionaries. Most of those countries were in the section of the world that was catching my eye at the time. Ralph Winter, founder of the US Center for World Mission—who was later listed as one of *Time* magazine's top twenty-five most influential evangelicals—turned the missions world upside down back in 1974 when he spoke at the first Lausanne Congress on World Evangelization. There he challenged leaders to look past the political borders of nation-states to strategize based on the great diversity of "unreached people groups" within those nations in order to reach the 2.4 billion people of the world.[3] Billy Graham echoed this charge when he said, "The whole church must be mobilized to bring the whole gospel to the whole world. This is our calling. These are our orders."[4]

In the early 1980s, David B. Barrett, then-editor of the *World Christian Encyclopedia*, focused on the area that was home to the least-evangelized people of the world and called it "World A." George Otis, Jr., focused on an "oval power center" that overlapped many of the core countries where the Holy Spirit was drawing my attention. Finally, a staple of the early '90s Christian library, *Operation World: A Day-to-Day Guide to*

Praying for the World, featured Patrick J. Johnstone's reflections on the "Resistant Belt," an area that was opposed and intolerant to the claims of Christ, the advance of the gospel, and those proclaiming it.

As I spoke at Lausanne II, I noted that most of the unreached people groups live in a belt that extends from West Africa across Asia, between the latitudes of 10 and 40 degrees north of the equator, an area including the Muslim, Hindu, and Buddhist blocks. Over the following twelve months, I carefully observed that particular part of the world, from both the outside and inside. We were a mere decade away from the year 2000, which seemed to many at that time to be a year of destiny. We sensed a *kairos*, a special moment from God, compelling us to concentrate our efforts on the most gospel-resistant region of the world, what we then called the 10/40 Box.

With all the energy of a stirring that was clearly from God, we continued to seek out ministries and organizations to join us with a vision for the year 2000. Soon, along with Lausanne's Thomas Wang and 350 leaders from the wider spectrum of the Christian world, we set up a small collaborative organization to multiply worldwide missions efforts in view of the pivotal year 2000. We called it AD2000 and set up office. In the first several months of 1989, AD2000 became the seedbed out of which a tiny shoot would spring up and grow into an unexpected tree. And like all trees, only God knew just how big it would grow.

A NEW VIEW

In July 1990, when I was presenting my findings at a Partners International annual event in beautiful Mt. Hermon, California,

Doris and I looked out the window to take in the sight of the stunning redwoods. Then we looked down at the plastic overhead projector page in our laps as we readied the materials for my presentation. Gazing back and forth between the redwoods and the see-through page in our laps, we began to think about a new way to frame that rectangle on the map, that "Resistant Belt" or "10/40 Box." With all our prayerful research, we were starting to see that geographic area not as something confining or impossible or boxlike, even, but as something hopeful, something you could see through, reach through, and even step through. We were starting to see it as an opportunity. This realization was a moment of crystal clarity: God had been training me, preparing me, and giving me the resources needed to partner with others for a new moment in missions history.

Beginning with my early days at Arthur Andersen, I had always had an interest in system design and computer programming. In my leadership role at Partners International, I had begun to look at how to take the information gathered by various Christian ministries and missions and connect them with innovative technological tools that had just become available. One of those technological tools was a brand-new mapping software. For the first time in history, it was possible to take a graph or table, input the data source, and immediately see the impact on a map.

Nowadays, we have a vast amount of technology at our fingertips and data that can be processed and displayed in a split second. But in the missions world at the time, communication was limited to phone calls and what we now call "snail mail." Remember when the CIA and FBI were doing their work in complete isolation of one another with no avenues of communication between? Or when Chicago's public transport existed as a scattering of disconnected lines owned by separate companies? The missions world had a similarly ineffective structure and mentality, meaning that many important ideas or pieces of information were not getting into the hands of the people who needed them most. We were doing our best to remedy that with meetings like Lausanne and organizations like the US Center for World Mission and publications like the *World Christian Encyclopedia,* but we had yet to see it all come together.

My contribution would come through technology, a tool my father had so often encouraged me to learn how to wield. I was like a kid playing a video game, typing in commands and searching every nook and cranny for some hidden key or treasure. In that era before well-known tech experts developed visually friendly operating systems for the world to use, I saw the black screen and prompts as a code to crack. Having my longtime love for computer programming paired with exciting new technology, I pulled information on poverty and ministry from sources in every country of the world, consulting all along with researcher Bob Waymire of Ralph Winter's US Center for World Mission. Late nights in my son's room, I would sit at the computer and tinker with the data. Other times, I would visit with experts at a secular mapping firm and piece things together.

One day as I visited software programmer Pete Holzmann at Strategic Mapping International, I asked him to help me create an accurate box on the map with the calculations from the data I had gathered. He typed some things in and within a few moments, I saw the spiritual data and material data overlaid, statistics settling into place one on top of the other. My fellow mission strategists and I had never before seen the connection. The map finally made it clear. Where there was physical poverty, there was also poverty of the gospel. Where people were starved for food or resources, there also happened to be a spiritual famine with little or no access to the message of Jesus. Like invisible ink seen only through special glasses, the truth was coming through: a low quality of life persisted where Christ was not named. The poorest of the poor and those least reached with the gospel were, according to the statistics, the very same people. After leaning on decades, even centuries, of work done by those Great Commission pioneers who came before, I was literally knocked off my feet in that moment of sudden realization in the mapping firm. Although I was in the middle of a secular institution, I couldn't help but collapse on the floor, get on my face, and thank the Lord for bringing this to light.

CATCHING ON

A few months later in 1990, I went back to Illinois to the largest student missions conference in the world, InterVarsity's Urbana. The atmosphere felt charged, electric. I shared the platform with my friend Anita Deyneka—then a director with the Slavic Gospel Association—who talked about what God was doing with students in the former Soviet Union, which had opened its Iron Curtain to the world just a few months earlier. As I came to the podium, I spoke from Colossians 1 on the lordship of Christ and how His transforming power seemed strangely absent in this region I was now calling the 10/40 Window.

At the end of the week, a group of students prepared a set of rap lyrics to sum up the content of the conference, and the "10/40 Window" suddenly became a catch phrase. After the conference, we started hearing it more and more in faith circles. People were using it in conversations. Soon *Christianity Today* picked up on the term in an article. People began to team up in a whole new way with a hope and a vision for reaching the unreached in the 10/40 Window. That very phrase turned out to be the water God used to grow that tiny, unexpected tree that was the AD2000 movement, with little to no resources, into something strong. God was moving and allowing us to lend words to His heart and vision for the poorest of the poor. Through the teamwork of missionaries and strategists that came before me, and the vibrant movement of young people who picked up the vision of the 10/40 Window, we witnessed a monumental shift in missions history.

THE BIG PICTURE

It's important to remember that the 10/40 Window concept didn't come out of nowhere. Missions history certainly didn't begin with me and my contemporaries. We would all be wise to recognize that the gospel didn't just fall into our laps by chance. When Doris and I responded to my brother's urging and began to first read Scripture back in our twenties, we were following a long line of people who had heard the message of Jesus from someone else who had heard the same message from someone else who had heard from someone else. God has employed a long line of pioneering leaders, well-known or unknown, to reach each of us where we are.

We go way back to a core of eleven followers and the growing church in Jerusalem sent out to be witnesses by the power of the Holy Spirit promised by Jesus when He ascended into glory. Before that, a courageous line of Old Testament history makers anticipated the first coming of Christ, keeping the faith when it had not yet become sight. God tells us in Hebrews 12:1 that a great cloud of witnesses cheers on the next era of believers from their place in glory. They've run their race; now we're running ours. As we grow tired or distracted by the concerns of everyday life, weighed down by sin or circumstance, the example and encouragement of previous generations can help us gain new resolve to cut loose from what holds us back and to put our shoes to the ground. God has worked mightily through generations past. Those stories in church history have a bearing on what He wants to do in our day.

My guess is if you're reading this book, you want to find a way to act out your faith, connect with others, and make a positive impact on a broken world. Maybe deep down you care about the needs around the globe, but you're overwhelmed and overworked by the needs in your own home. Maybe you've got First-World guilt or compassion fatigue. Maybe you're running tired in the hamster wheel of a demanding work schedule, a "just get by" family life, and the unending, never-satisfying scroll of social media. Your chest tightens at the thought of racial tension, arguments over refugee care, food scarcity, and unwanted babies. You want to do more, but you can't seem to get your bearings.

These feelings are not new or unique to you. Era after era, believers in Jesus have longed for an ideal but felt pulled to keep doing things the way everyone else does them. In your struggle, I encourage you to follow the advice in Job 8:8, one of the very few helpful pieces of advice given to Job while processing his difficulties. "For inquire, please, of bygone ages," Job's friend said, "and consider what the fathers have searched out." I encourage you to dig into the larger story of faith-sharing through the epochs and eras, and into the smaller narratives of your own personal history.

You have your own story of how a specific believer in a long line of others handed the gospel to you like a relay baton. A grandmother who prayed for you, an ancestor who endured persecution and lived to tell you their testimony, a pastor who rightly divided the Word of truth and spoke it with grace to you, a believer who left the comforts of their own home to learn your language and live out the gospel in your great-grandparents' distant town, a friend who studied the Bible with you in your days at the university. What if any of those people had said no to God's invitation to follow Jesus and join His mission? What would that have meant for your life? Think back on the sequence of events and the various people God has used to draw you to Himself. Then think about all the Christians before them who were faithful in handing down the gospel. Dig into church history. Start with the book of Acts and Hebrews 11, and then read about the spread of the gospel all the way to the movements in recent eras. Search out the stories of those who've gone before, and they'll teach you how to step out of the hamster wheel to find a more effective way of life.

Over the forty-four years that I've been following the Lord, He has continually turned my head to notice the remarkable work He's set in motion. He has introduced me to past generations who pioneered missions in a time when traveling to foreign lands might mean never seeing your family members again. He has shown me those faithful workers just ahead of me in the journey, allowing me to springboard from their ideas and help believers in Jesus know where and how to follow the call God has given them. And He has shown me a whole crowd of ordinary people who are saying yes to God, watching extraordinary stories unfold in their small circles of influence.

In the chapters to come, you'll read stories of believers who have taken time to understand God's vision for the unreached areas of the world, those who have stepped out of their *status quo* lives in whatever country they call home to say yes to something, and Someone, beyond themselves. As these adventurers have taken time to rethink their way of life, they have searched for what it means to be a good neighbor to those on their street or on the other side of the world. They've taken care of refugees, brought peace amid ethnic tension, stamped out the stigma of the orphan, and ministered to the tired working class. They've seen an opening to make an impact and they've said yes. God desires something similar for you. Second Corinthians 1:20 says, "For all the promises of God find their Yes in him. That is why it is through him that we utter our Amen to God for his glory." Every promise from God is an invitation to believe and act. When we take Him at His word and step forward in obedience, good things are sure to come, things that will warrant a hearty "Amen!"

Each chapter that follows will share a step in the process of transformation I call "The Yes Effect." This is a particular type of transformation that my friends and ministry partners have seen consistently in their own lives and in the world as a result of accepting God's repeated invitations to activate their faith in new ways. True transformation is sparked when we reorient our hearts, get in sync with God's tenderness toward the oppressed, and regain compassion for the lost. We let the Lord work in us, and then we can't help but join the work He is doing in the world around us.

While the attitudes and approaches in the stories of this book are indeed inspiring, God doesn't want your life to be a replica of others' lives. Many of the examples in these stories might seem unusual, unattainable, or even unrealistic from the point of view of your everyday life. That's okay. What might seem exotic to you is simply everyday life for someone else. So don't discount who and where you are as you read on. God has a plan for every latitude and longitude on the globe. Just because your story doesn't sound exactly like the ones in this book doesn't mean God's not writing it.

The examples in this book are meant to encourage you and show you that no matter the context, when a follower of Jesus says yes to His invitation, all kinds of possibilities open up in that particular person's life in that particular corner of the world. Wherever and whoever you are, God is inviting you to expand the goodness of His kingdom on earth as it is in heaven. He is inviting you to rethink your way of life and step out into something new. He is inviting you to watch the most beautiful chain reactions of transformation unfold as a result of saying yes to Him, even in the smallest of ways. That's the Yes Effect.

As Paul says in 1 Corinthians 11:1 (NIV), "Follow my example, as I follow the example of Christ." Each of us comes after a long line of committed followers of Christ who have shown us how the life of faith is done. Just as generations of city planners added their various insights and solutions to build the infrastructure of my home city, Chicago, so have generations of passionate believers in Jesus offered their gifting and heart for service, co-laboring with God to grow His kingdom. Imagine what could happen if we learn from those in the generation before us and build upon their work, if we carry on the legacy of the past instead of letting it fade into modern apathy. I invite you to read on, take a look and see what God has been doing in cities and countries across the globe. Let the stories in these pages speak hope and urgency into your soul. Listen for God's invitation to join His transforming work in the world around you. And be ready to say yes.

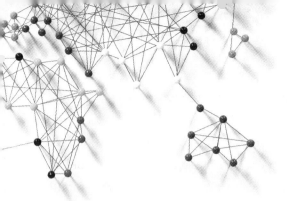

Open Your Heart

Working away at tasks in their shop, the little girl's parents had their backs turned. They didn't notice, but their two-year-old, Yue Yue, had toddled into the alley that cut through the middle of the hardware market in Guangdong Province, China. The tiny girl stood in the open space for a few moments, wide-eyed with curiosity, turning her head toward the big, bright sale signs hanging over entrances. Then she turned to look toward a stack of fat parcels of fabric bundled on the ground. While taking in the sights of the alley, she didn't see the danger coming for her.

A white van speeding down the lane hit Yue Yue head-on, knocking her to the concrete and rolling over her with one of its front tires. Inexplicably, the driver then hit the brakes, put the van into reverse, and moved back a few inches before shifting back into drive. He hit the gas to move forward, sadly rolling over the little girl's body again, before finally driving away.

In the minutes that followed, a middle-aged man began walking toward Yue Yue. Somehow she was still breathing. Yet he stepped around, keeping his eyes from meeting those of the crumpled girl on the ground. From the other direction, a man on a motor scooter zipped across the alley, changing his course to avoid the severely wounded toddler. Seemingly invisible, she lay there as yet another pedestrian passed her by, not looking, not stopping, not daring even to move her out of the middle of the street.

Then further harm came. This time around, it took on the form of a truck. Without slowing or swerving, the driver rolled his tires right over the little girl. Yue Yue moved her arms as if to wave for help. She needed someone to see her, to care, to come. Instead, her fellow citizens passed by her, hardly giving a second glance.

There was a man in a motorized rickshaw, another driving a bicycle cart, another on a scooter, another steering a rickshaw loaded with cardboard scraps, another on a motorcycle. All who approached drove right on by, leaving the little wounded person sprawled on the street like worthless garbage. A second motorcyclist, this one wearing a cape, passed between the crumpled girl and a child holding hands with her mother. The caped man, another could-be hero, came back again to look at the crushed child—three times. But he failed to reach out to the girl, to look for her parents, or to call for help. Hope was fading—fast. If not a hero with a cape, then who?

After yet another man walked by, the long-awaited hero finally walked onto the scene. But this hero wasn't wearing a cape. This hero didn't have an insignia popping out on top of superhuman muscles. In fact, this hero didn't seem to have many muscles at all. This hero was just an old woman, a trash collector, walking into the alley to do her job. She was an un-likely hero perhaps, but a hero nonetheless. When it came down to it, she was the only one who could tell the difference between Yue Yue and the trash.

The woman stopped in the middle of the now-quiet street, a bag of garbage still in hand, and she stared over at Yue Yue from some distance. Almost in slow motion, she placed the bag of garbage into her pile and looked around, seemingly puzzled and dismayed that no one else had seen this wounded child on the road and had come to her aid. With her hands now freed, the trash lady walked over to the girl and stood over her with shocked urgency. Yue Yue, somehow still alive, turned her body with what little motion she had left, desperately grasped at her head, and looked up at the woman.[1]

"I was picking up trash in the hardware market when I saw a child lying in the road," Chen Xianmei, said in an interview with *China Daily.* "I walked up in a hurry to the girl and heard her groan. I lifted her up and saw that one of her eyes was closed, that she had tears in her eyes, and she was bleeding from her mouth, nose and the back of her head." As Chen reached down to pick up Yue Yue, she hesitated slightly, feeling the child's body collapse from the broken bones and whatever other internal injuries she had sustained. Finally, Chen decided to carefully drag Yue Yue out of harm's way, and place her next to the parcels on the side of the lane so she could go find more help.[2] Yue Yue made it to the Guangdong Military Hospital, but after a week in a coma, her tiny heart stopped.[3]

Each of the eighteen people who passed by Yue Yue either denied seeing her or confessed to being too afraid to step in to help. Yue Yue may have had a chance at surviving if one of the earlier passersby had cared enough to do what Chen had done.[4] From the time the surveillance footage first made rounds through Chinese social media and then circled the globe, there has been much scrutiny from citizens of the world, and soul-searching within China itself, about what kind of society China has become that at least eighteen witnesses would turn a blind eye to an injured, dying child.

IN THE DUMPS

Most of us would say we'd never walk by a wounded child and leave her for dead. But we may neglect the wounded in smaller ways. Maybe because we know our consciences are still sensitive enough to feel that punch in the gut when we come across sad situations, we instead try to insulate ourselves, to keep ourselves from seeing or knowing. We subconsciously keep ourselves from coming near so we don't have to wrestle with the discomfort of helping. The busyness of daily routines at home; the unrelenting schedules of school, work, and even church; overstimulation from too much media; the overwhelming need in far-off places and feeling like there's no practical way to help—all of these can numb us to the plight of others.

Psalm 138:6 tells us, "For though the LORD is high, he regards the lowly, but the haughty he knows from afar." God sees and hears the wounded and lowly, and He wants us to see and hear them, too. "Whoever closes his ear to the cry of the poor will himself call out and not be answered," Proverbs 21:13 says. God invites us to tune our hearts. He urges us to see, hear, and feel for the lowly.

What traumas or tragedies have you stumbled across lately? Whether a friend's loved one passing, a refugee whose family has been separated in war zones, a shooting in an urban neighborhood, a neighbor battling an extended illness, a couple fighting for their marriage, an overextended single mom struggling to balance her responsibilities—what has been your first inclination or response? Have you spent time searching out the details of the situation to truly understand the depths of it? Have you tuned in with the Lord and sensed His care for the people involved? Or have you felt the initial, momentary sting and, in a fit of spiritual attention deficit disorder, moved on to the next bit of information with each new stimulus helping you forget the last?

In telling the story of the Good Samaritan, Jesus says, "But a Samaritan, as he journeyed, came to where he was, and when he saw him, he had compassion" (Luke 10:33). The Greek word (*splagchnizomai*) translated as "compassion" here denotes being overcome with raw emotion that exhibits itself as physical discomfort. Literally, it means "to be moved as to one's bowels," or to have your guts wrenched by what you see, to be sick to your stomach, even to double over in feeling someone else's pain.[5] You likely experienced that when you read about Yue Yue.

But many of us put up blinders to keep from coming across things that would punch us in the gut. Or we scurry on to something more pleasant when we accidentally come across things that hurt. But tuning in to the heart of God involves sitting for an extended period of time with one thing or one person in need. It involves submitting to discomfort and growing not just in sympathy, which cares from a distance, but empathy, which feels and relates from within our personal experience of pain.

I experienced that gut-wrenching feeling the first time I visited the Manila dump community in the Philippines. I had stopped over in the city on my way to participate in the 1986 World Evangelical Fellowship General Assembly in Singapore. That day, I walked alongside Andrew, an eighteen-year-old who for two years had been serving in the community of some seven thousand garbage dump residents who made their living from collecting and selling scraps. Methane gas hovered in a cloud over one-room shacks built from corrugated metal, sheets of thick plastic, and plywood salvaged from the dump. I continually brought my hand up to my face to filter out some of the odor. I found it difficult to stomach that people actually lived in those makeshift structures in this putrid air. Worse than that, residents of the dump actually swam in the toxic water of the polluted river flowing into the Pacific.

As I got brave, put on my boots, and hiked the heaps of smoldering refuse with Andrew, a wailing woman approached us. In her hand, she carried a trash bag that contained the remains of her infant baby who had recently died. Without the money to give the baby a decent burial, she approached Andrew, desperate for help.

What a graphic picture of our world, even if it's not the world we know on an everyday, personal level. It can be easy to ignore those in need when we see them from the safety and insulation of our own bubble, and easier still to ignore them when we don't see them at all. But the need is real. In a rapidly growing urban world, which is increasingly unfriendly, we need to mobilize all who believe in Christ in every country of the globe to bring the good news to desperate people. In order to mobilize, we believers in Jesus must first feel the urgency of the task. And in order to feel the urgency of the task, we must simply be willing to feel. Will we say yes?

THE DISCARDED

In every worthy story, a character stumbles upon a crisis and is forced to choose between compassion and callousness, courage and cowardice. One's choice determines whether one will be considered a hero. Not all of us are confronted with such dramatic opportunities like those of the Chinese garbage collector or the Good Samaritan to test our inner self. And often, we actually prefer to remain unchallenged. We try to stay safe and happy, ignoring the reality of unpleasant situations in places out of sight. But we do not have to live this way. Jesus said, "Learn from me, for I am gentle and lowly in heart" (Matt. 11:29). We can find a way out of our go-to defense mechanisms and self-focused behaviors. There is hope for change when we look to the Lord, and the older generations He's placed before us, as our teacher.

In Isaiah 1:17, the Lord affirms that those of us who haven't actively embraced the lowly can "learn to do good; seek justice, correct oppression; bring justice to the fatherless, plead the widow's cause." This kind of compassion isn't reserved for a special kind of person, a missionary or a pastor or a monk. This kind of compassion can be learned. When we don't naturally feel the desire to correct oppression, we can learn to. When we don't naturally tend toward pleading the cause of the under-privileged, we can learn to.

So it was for a man whom many in Cairo, Egypt, now know as Father Sama'an. In his young adulthood, when he was known as Brother Farahat, there were pockets of poverty in certain areas of the city where free-roaming chickens pecked through piles of garbage on dirt alleys, but for the most part, life for him was tidy and comfortable. He worked a regular job and volunteered at a well-established Coptic Orthodox church in his free time. But there was more for him to learn. And that meant he was about to experience change, which would come by yet another trash collector.

This trash collector's name was Qidees. From the outskirts of the city where a group of people called the Zabbaleen lived, Qidees came with his cart every day to gather the rubbish from Father Sama'an's street. Feeling the Holy Spirit's prompting, Father Sama'an began to share the good news of Jesus with Qidees, whose name happened to mean "Saint." As their talks grew longer and more frequent, Father Sama'an invited Qidees into his home to continue the conversation. Qidees was drawn to the gospel and soon he confessed his sin and accepted Jesus as his Savior.

As he grew in knowledge and love of the Lord, Qidees looked with compassion over his people, the Zabbaleen, and his neighborhood, known as "Garbage City." He peeked into the stalls thick with pig slop. He walked with the gamblers, drug abusers, alcoholics, and aggressors. He ached at the brokenness of his people. Soon, he began to share his heavy heart with Father Sama'an. Day after day, he brought his plea,

"Come and tell my people about Jesus."[6] For two whole years, from 1972 to 1974, he gave the same invitation. He would not relent. Finally, Father Sama'an got the sense that this invitation wasn't coming from a man, but through a man and from God.

One Friday at the beginning of March, as Qidees begged yet again, Father Sama'an sensed the Lord say, "I'm the One who's calling you. Go with this man."[7] He agreed to meet Qidees after work that evening. But there was a strong pull against the call. As Father Sama'an went to Ramses Square to catch a bus to the meeting point, he began having second thoughts and found himself boarding a bus in the opposite direction. After two stops, he could not resist the pinch of the Holy Spirit trying to get his attention. The bus tilted to one side as it circled a roundabout. He was like Jonah on the ship toward anywhere but Ninevah. Father Sama'an knew how that story ended. And so, once and for all, he obeyed and got off at the next stop to turn around and go toward Qidees, toward Garbage City, toward God's heart.

They walked for a long time, past the shacks made of used-up metal. Walls of garbage loomed around them. Father Sama'an, having grown up as a farmer's son, was used to the smell of the barn, but even with such training, his lungs could hardly handle the sickening stench of Garbage City. It's not surprising that many in the area were physically ill. Toxins from the garbage and sewage seeped into the groundwater and then into the bodies of the people who drank it in. But the damage didn't stop there. The community had astronomical percentages of addiction to alcohol, gambling, and drugs. There in the middle of rotten food, scrap materials, and filth, Father Sama'an saw a group of people who themselves had been discarded like trash. What had broken the heart of the garbage collector Qidees was now breaking the heart of Father Sama'an.

IRON FISTS, IRON HEARTS

In the story of the Good Samaritan, the unlikely hero bandages the victim, likely tearing his own clothes to use as a tourniquet on open wounds. He pours his own wine and oil to sterilize and soothe the man's wounds. He puts the man on his own beast, carries him to an inn, and stays overnight to care for him. When he must be on his way and can stay no more, he gives his own money to the innkeeper for continued care until he can return to check on the patient. Only then, after doing all this, does the Samaritan get back to his original journey. Though ignoring the man and continuing on his way might have been the convenient and less costly thing to do, one whose heart beats like God's heart cannot turn away from those who are suffering. In sharing this parable, Jesus communicates that a good neighbor stops what he's doing and goes out of his way to help, even using his own resources and finances to heal the wound. If we don't see our neighbors and fellow citizens of the world in the same tender way that Jesus does, we need to let Him work on our hearts. God wants to break our heart of stone and give us a heart of flesh so we can feel what He feels. God knows that when we don't allow ourselves to feel, we become too hardened to act.

When the Iron Curtain of the Soviet Union began to fall in 1989, the impact of long-term crackdowns on religious expression left behind a bedraggled and calloused population. As the government spoon-fed communism to its people and allowed for no other intake, iron seemed to flow through the spiritual veins of many citizens. Hearts were hardened. Cut off from knowledge of their loving Creator, many citizens were only shells of what they were meant to be. They were Stalin-like on the exterior while wasting away inside. The Iron Curtain may have fallen in the political world, but in many cases, it still had a hold on the hearts of those who had lived under its tight-fisted control.

In Ukraine, where my friend Steve Weber has lived and worked since 1991, one particular subgroup of the population felt the brunt of this hard-heartedness. Orphans, by no fault of their own, were considered the lowest rung on the societal ladder, mere cast-offs to ignore and avoid. The regular population seemed to have an unspoken assumption that the orphans' plight in life had more to do with some defect within them than with an unfortunate sequence of events that happened to them. As the iron-hearted system prohibited these vulnerable children from grasping the rungs above them for upward mobility, they were treated as if being abandoned by one's parents is some sort of highly contagious disease. In fact, they were segregated. The government provided separate institutions of education for orphans to prevent them from bringing any ill effect upon the rest of the children of Ukrainian or Russian society.

"Orphans were considered bad blood, bad genes, bad everything," Steve said.[8] Even Christians who had a desire to adopt an orphan faced almost insurmountable social stigma. Those who chose to adopt would often hide their decision from friends and family to avoid the resulting ridicule. Often a woman preparing to adopt would feign being pregnant by sliding a pillow under her shirt for the three months leading up to an adoption so that no one would suspect her child had once been an orphan.

Yet, as Steve says, God has a plan for the orphan. That plan is adoption. As Psalm 68:5–6 tells us, "a father of the fatherless," our God "places the solitary in families *and* gives the desolate a home in which to dwell" (AMPC). How does God do this? By using people. His people of faith must resist the peer pressure of society and embrace the father heart of God.

Many orphanages help alleviate some suffering, but as another advocate for adoption, my longtime friend Anita Deyneka, points out, "In one survey of orphanages in Russia, only ten percent of orphans grew up to lead successful lives. Heartbreakingly, ten percent committed suicide. The remainder became criminals, prostitutes, human trafficking victims, or drug addicts. It's very bleak. But we can see an extraordinary difference when children are adopted into caring families."[9]

As we look back at the story of the Good Samaritan and picture the Jewish priest and the Levite (an assistant priest, himself) coming upon the sight of a dying man on the road to Jericho, we expect that their training in the temple and their study of God's character will lead them to kneel down and tend to the victim. But it is not so with them. Whether they are afraid of being soiled by the dying man's uncleanness, of putting themselves in danger of robbers who may still be lurking, or of intervening in what could look to them like a punishment from God that this man deserves, the two travelers not only pass by the victim, but also distance themselves from his body to get the least exposed to it as possible. And we could be left wondering, if not a priest or an assistant priest, then who? As in the case of little Yue Yue, sometimes the "who" doesn't look like we would expect.

When a rescuer finally comes to the dying man on the road to Jericho, he is what would have been considered by many locals to be scum of the earth, a half-bred heretic Samaritan. In fact, as you may have heard in a sermon or two in your own church, most Jews on their way to Jerusalem would do everything they could to avoid walking through Samaria and getting its dust on their feet. It is this traveler from the lowest rung of society, one who is considered a second-class citizen, who sees the victim. Instead of looking at him in shame or disgust or turning the other way, he looks on him with compassion, a compassion that quickly leads to a rescue effort. Real compassion is active. We take on God's heart when we refuse to look away.

BE MOVED

My friend Linda, who supports efforts to end human trafficking around the world, tells the sad plight of men who come from places like Bangladesh or the Philippines to seek work in Dubai, maybe a construction or factory job. Their handlers ask for their passports and papers, and never give them back. The handlers make good money by inserting new photos and selling the passports on the black market. Later, it looks like the victim left Dubai on a certain date while, in fact, he ends up homeless on Dubai's streets.[10]

In other real-life scenarios, women from Moldova, Ukraine, Georgia, and other parts of Eastern Europe answer an ad for a secretarial job, get off the plane in Berlin, are taken to an apartment, forced to give up their passport, and are raped repeatedly for forty-eight hours until their spirits and bodies are broken. After the women endure that ordeal, their handlers send them to brothels and threaten them saying, "We know what village you're from, your mother's name, your daughter's name."[11] Without a passport or anyone to intervene, these women hold little hope for freedom and returning home.

We need only to hear these stories to be moved, to experience that sinking feeling in our stomachs, to feel the stirring of compassion for our fellow humans. Many missionaries say that they didn't go to their countries of service with the specific task of fighting human trafficking, or some other tragedy, but that the issue simply landed in their laps as they went about serving in their formal areas of ministry, and that they found they just couldn't turn away from the plight of these victims.

But the problem for the average citizen is that these stories are less often shared than those more wholesome and inspiring accounts from the mission field. Run-ins with the trafficking industry have been glossed over or edited out of many missionaries' reports during furlough visits to the United States over the years as the average churchgoer may not be able to stomach it. But how else are we to develop compassion for a people who are invisible to us, those who don't have a voice?

In the 1990s, justice proponents in the U.S. began to look more closely at this dark industry that has a foothold in so many communities of the 10/40 Window, and even right here in the States. Soon after, anti-human-trafficking experts convened congressional hearings and drafted our nation's first law against human trafficking. As the issue has drawn more attention and public outcry has increased, nonprofit organizations with expertise in this area have popped up all over the country, training citizens to recognize the tactics of traffickers, communicating protocol for when a situation seems sinister, and teaching volunteers how to find the right help for victims.[12]

For far too long, this issue remained hidden in dark places. But as brave rescue workers and victims have come out from the shadows to tell their stories, more and more volunteers have felt their hearts beat strongly for the well-being of the victim, gaining courage to stand up and devote themselves to the good fight. We must see, know, and feel to fully take in the urgency of the situations around us. Will you passively remain segregated, insulated from those who need a hand up and out of their plight? Or will you engage your senses and allow yourself to be moved?

UNDER THE RUBBLE

Atop of a heap of rubble, a team of men in hardhats drilled, pulled, and pried away broken pieces of cement. Earlier that day, war planes had dropped bombs on civilian territories in Idlib, Syria, killing more than a dozen people and trapping many others in the debris of collapsed buildings. After hours of digging, a rescue worker lifted a baby girl up from the ashes. Quickly, Abu Kifah rushed the girl down to the ambulance where the crowd erupted in shouts and applause.[13] As they shuttled her to the hospital and emergency personnel began to wipe away the soot from her remarkably minimal wounds, Abu Kifah clutched the baby and broke into deep, guttural sobs. "When I carried her I felt like she was my daughter," he said. "She moved me deeply." In a tender gesture, the baby looked him in the eye, batted at his jacket, and reached for his face.[14] Released by Syria Civil Defense, the video of Abu Kifah's heart-wrenching reaction went viral, bringing citizens all over the world, and even a prominent journalist, to weep along with him. If we are too far away to understand the gravity of a situation, or too overstimulated by statistical reports, or overwhelmed by the hopelessness of a war zone, seeing raw emotion in someone else can help us dig down to the parts of our heart beneath the rubble. Under a heart of stone, we can once again find a heart of flesh.

Often people ask my friend Linda and her fellow workers in the struggle against human trafficking, "Why would you put yourself in such a dangerous place? Why would you reach out to these people? They're so lost."[15] I'm sure Abu Kifah and his fellow rescuers have answered similar questions. Hopelessness and unchecked fear petrify us, harden our hearts, and leave us too tense to help the wounded and weary. But this video of a tiny survivor, and of the man who wept over her, shows us what it looks like to fully feel in the midst of things that could callous us. What a poignant picture for the believer in Jesus. He invites us to sift through the mess and discover something priceless. Though we are surrounded by destruction, there is treasure buried beneath debris, something of infinite value that we must unearth.

NO LOST CAUSES

God invites us to stoop low, to get close enough to feel the pain of society's throwaways and lost causes. Those who are trash in the culture's eyes are treasure to Him, and they're worth seeking and saving.

Is your heart more often a heart of stone or of flesh? How have you insulated yourself from feeling the pain of others in dire need? How might you dig through the rubble to find that place of deep feeling and empathy? I encourage you to focus on one event, person, or issue that has pricked a strong response in you recently. Look up a few articles, photos, audio recordings, or videos about that event, person, or issue that can help you become more compassionate. Write down any words that come to mind that describe the plight of that person or place. Save a screenshot or sketch an image that captures your heart for that situation. Wouldn't it be great if, instead of flitting from one thing to another and becoming desensitized to the most dire needs around us, we would stop and attend to the pain of one person or place? As we continue our journey through this book, keep that one person, place, or problem in mind and consider how God might be inviting you into that context to be an agent of transformation.

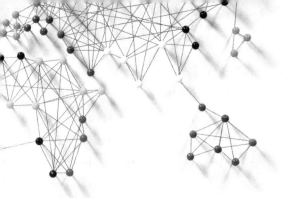

Fix Your Eyes

Through the dust and muck of Garbage City, donkey-drawn carts hauled in what the lucky ones in other parts of Cairo had thrown away. Father Sama'an, or Brother Farahat as he was known at the time, noticed the bloodshot eyes of addicts and the withering bodies of the sick, those slowly fading away from overexposure to toxic fumes and polluted water. The smell alone was barely manageable, but the sight of it all felt like more than he could bear. "I can't help these people," Father Sama'an sighed under his breath. Sure, he could ride the bus back home to his comfortable apartment, but he could never unsee this.[1]

Exposure to overwhelming need can make our hearts feel paralyzed. We may feel like taking a sick day, or a sick year to sort it all out. We feel powerless to change the scene. And we are powerless on our own. In these moments, whether as an individual or a team, we must acknowledge that the very problems we want to tackle could very well tackle us if we don't look at them with the right perspective. The only way to get a proper look is to do what is counterintuitive: close our eyes.

Through His prophet Isaiah, the Lord said to His people, "In returning and rest you shall be saved; in quietness and in trust shall be your strength" (Isa. 30:15). To move forward in a healthy way, we must take a breather from the chaos around us—not to ignore it or insulate ourselves, but rather to process it with the Lord. With knowledge of the complicated issues before us, we choose to rest in and trust God. As we surrender, God does something amazing: He takes our burdens and transforms them into passions. This is when even the heaviest and hardest barriers begin to budge.

THE MOUNTAIN THAT MOVED

Instead of looking down at what he saw in Garbage City, Father Sama'an decided to look up. There, a small mountain towered above the district's filth. The name of the mountain, Mokattam, literally means "broken off." As Father Sama'an looked up at Mokattam, he thought about the testimony of what happened there centuries earlier, the miracle that came when God's people closed their eyes to the troubles of the world and took them to the Lord in prayer.

He remembered the story of the Muslim caliph in the tenth century who often invited Muslims, Christians, and Jews to debate the veracity of their respective faiths. While the debates had generally been friendly, one government official began searching the New Testament—not to learn of Jesus, but to find a way to trap the Coptic Orthodox Pope and humiliate the Christians of Cairo. Seventeen chapters in, he found his ammunition: "Truly I tell you, if you have faith as small as a mustard seed, you can say to this mountain, 'Move from here to there,' and it will move. Nothing will be impossible for you" (Matt. 17:20 NIV). He scoffed at the thought. The official then eyed the mountain on the edge of the city and schemed with the caliph, persuading him to demand that the Christians prove their faith and move the mountain. The Christians had four options: they could perform the miracle and prove Christianity to be true; they could abandon Christianity on account of it being invalid and become Muslims instead; or if they failed to produce the miracle, they could choose between leaving Egypt to become exiles or taking death by sword.

The Christians requested three days reprieve and rallied together in their local sanctuary. There they closed their eyes to the discord, threats, and seemingly impossible odds before them. They fasted and prayed. For three days, they paused their schedules and stayed in the "Suspended Church" in Old Cairo. They waited for a word from the Lord. After dozing off in prayer, the pope received a message in a dream. He later followed the strange instructions he had received: he looked for a one-eyed man carrying water near the iron gate in the market place.

This one-eyed man, Sama'an—after whom Brother Farahat would eventually be named—was a shoemaker, a simple man. He had very literally followed the teaching of Jesus that if you lust with your eyes, it would be better to pluck one of them out than to lose your soul and walk with full sight into an eternity separated from God. As part of his morning routine, the half-blind man filled his water flask to take to the sick and elderly who could not come to fetch water for themselves. This devoted follower of Jesus, who had permanently closed one of his eyes to the temptations of the world, was the one chosen to help his fellow believers face the taunting crowd of unbelievers. His strategy? The Christians would close their eyes to the temptations and threats around them. They would publicly plead for the Lord's mercy. They would worship God in sight of the skeptics. They would fix their gaze on the Lord and trust Him to turn their faith into sight.

Soon the day of decision came. One-eyed Sama'an and the pope led the crowd of believers up the mountain with their incense, candles, crosses, and Bibles. They brought church to the mountain. There, they worshiped the Lord in front of the Muslim caliph and the unbelieving crowds who gathered to gawk at what would become of the Christians. The Christians began confessing their sin with a broken heart and a crushed spirit, shouting out the famous liturgical prayer, Kyrie Eleison, "Lord, have mercy." They repeated the prayer one hundred times north, south, east, and west. Then, silence. As writer Bishop Mattaos so beautifully describes, these believers stood still "for a moment between the hands of the Most High."[2]

After that, Sama'an and the whole mass of Christians began to stand and then fall in worship—repeatedly. The pope stood by, touched his hand to his head, then his chest, then each shoulder in the sign of the cross. It is said that at this point, the solid ground beneath them began to lift up, broken from its base. As the Christians fell in worship, the mountain thrust downward. As they rose up again, so did the mountain, so much so that witnesses could see the sun through the middle, like a window to the other side. The mountain was moving, not out of the way as the caliph had hoped, but it was indeed moving. These followers of Jesus repeated the vertical motion three times until the caliph asked them to stop because they were shaking the whole city.

ON A WIND AND A PRAYER

As Father Sama'an's senses took in the details of the dire scene before him in Garbage City, the ancient story of the broken mountain kept him from returning to his comfortable apartment. Yet, as he looked around at the garbage people in that dump, smelled the odor of the city, and stood in its filth, he told the crowd, "I can do nothing to help you." He knew the Lord had told him to come to this forsaken place, yet he stood there traumatized by the great need he was witnessing. He didn't know what to do, but he knew the One who did. "I can do nothing to help you," he went on to complete his sentence, "except to start praying in this place."[3]

That spirit of prayer, directed toward the One who knows all and can do all, helped Father Sama'an break his feeling of paralysis and start to move. He arranged to meet with Qidees two days later on a Sunday morning. The need around him was too much for human eyes to take in, so Father Sama'an thought back on the legendary one-eyed man and the Christians who prayed on Mokattam. He knew God had met with His people at Mokattam in times past, so he looked up at the mountain and climbed it. Halfway up, he closed his eyes to the impossible scene below and began to listen. He began to expect. And that's when he found the opening of a long-forgotten cave where the monks used to pray and worship.

For three consecutive Sundays, Father Sama'an prayed there from morning to evening: *Why have You brought me here, Lord?*

What do You want me to do here? Tell me Your will for this place.
On the third Sunday, he took two people with him and prayed
until the sun started to set. Then, as darkness closed in, a storm
began brewing. The wind whipped around, pushing Father
Sama'an and billowing in his ears, muffling the sounds of the
city below. Dust stirred all around. He shielded his face with
his hands. Soon, discarded magazines and office papers soared
high up into the air. Pieces of cardboard and plastic hopped
about, as if the very breath of God had brought them to life. It
seemed everything in Garbage City was rising up.

The wind lifted up crumpled bits of trash, whirled them
around in the air, and tossed them up as high as Father Sama'an's
vantage point on the mountainside. He squinted his eyes and
coughed into his hands. Papers continued to fly higher, indis-
cernible from the birds in the sky. And out of the thousands of
papers that rose up from below, one single sheet floated down to
settle itself on the rock where Father Sama'an had knelt. Then,
the whipping wind calmed down to a gentle breeze.

Father Sama'an's friend reached out to pick up the piece of
paper from the ground. It was a page from a Bible. As the last
bit of sunlight shone on the mountainside, they opened their
eyes to the Word of God on the thin page in front of them:
"And the Lord said to Paul one night in a vision, 'Do not be
afraid, but go on speaking and do not be silent, for I am with
you, and no one will attack you to harm you, for I have many
in this city who are my people'" (Acts 18:9–10). Father Sama'an looked at the cave where people of God in ages past had
come to pray. He looked down below at the dwelling places
constructed of spare parts. And suddenly, he sensed in his spirit

that God wanted the citizens of Garbage City themselves to rise up and pray on this holy mountain. One day they would build a sanctuary in that sacred space. He could see it.

A MAP UNFOLDING

Many leaders in the faith have climbed up to desolate places to better hear God speak into the seemingly impossible situations in their lives and ministries. John the Baptist went to the wilderness to prepare himself before preparing the way for the Lord. Paul went away to the wilderness for a few years before embarking on his world-changing missionary journeys. And Jesus Himself went to the wilderness to be tempted before starting His public ministry. Later, as He visited the sick and needy in town after town, He continued to find time to escape the crowds and seek out isolated, quiet places to spend time in solitude and communion with the Father. If we want to see true transformation in the world, we must see the need in front of us through the filter of God's wisdom. We must listen and work in tandem with God, moving forward not in our own easily squelched eagerness, but with the inextinguishable compassion and vigor of the Holy Spirit.

Perhaps no one I know lives out this lifestyle of prayer more consistently than my friends Iman and Lea Santoso. Iman came to know the Lord during the great prayer revival that swept through Indonesia in the late 1960s and early '70s. In that era, nations sat on the edge of their seats waiting to see whether the Indonesian government would fall to communism. And in the midst of trouble, Iman, his friends, and the people of Indonesia as a whole were all ears to the hope of Jesus.

During a retreat that Iman attended, one of the speakers asked the participants to return to their rooms in absolute silence to pray, not talking to anyone on the way, so as to be fully focused on the presence of the Lord. As he prayed, Iman saw a vision of the map of Indonesia. On the map, Iman saw many islands laid out before him. Men and women came up from the islands, crying for help. God was speaking to Iman, speaking in him. He recalls:

> The Holy Spirit cried in me. I began to understand the love of God for humankind. You can't imagine that kind of love. Tremendous love. I hadn't had the proper burden for my Indonesian countrymen before then, but I followed the Holy Spirit and began to cry, too, wanting to see them saved. I wept for two hours, and then the map disappeared, as if washed away by tears. At that moment, I gave my life to see that this vision would be fulfilled. I knew this was from God.[4]

Indonesia, a nation with nearly eight hundred people groups[5] scattered over 6,000 inhabited islands[6] has dealt with its share of conflicts and violent takeover attempts between political parties and religious groups. From Iman's time in prayer and looking at the spiritual climate in his nation, he has sensed that in order for Indonesia to experience peace and wholeness as a nation of great diversity, there first would need to be a synergy among believers in Jesus.

With this hope in their hearts, every few months over the years, Iman and Lea have been leaving the noise and chaos of their city and taking a trip to the mountains to better hear from the Lord.

On one particular trip to the mountains, Iman was searching out God's guidance for where he should step out in ministry, how he should be involved as an individual in God's far-reaching plan for his nation and the world. Iman was a medical student at the time, doing his internships and practicing with patients. Then, as he continued to press on toward getting his medical license, the laboratory at his university burned down in the communist coup. Around him, his countrymen attacked one another with both words and weapons. He couldn't shake the thought that Indonesia desperately needed transformation. And that meant changes for Iman, too.

ON THE ROSTER

Step by step, Iman and Lea followed the Lord together. Each installment of His plan for them was revealed just before they'd need to make a move, like the light of a lantern shining at their feet. As Iman studied at a theological school, he began to sense that the Lord wanted to raise up a student movement in Indonesia through InterVarsity. Next, he and Lea sensed that they needed to travel all over the islands of Indonesia to recruit students. They didn't have the resources. Still, the Lord told them to go.

Suddenly, as they prepared, not knowing how they would get to where God wanted them to be, an old pastor noticed the Santosos' energetic faith. "I can't be as active at my age," he told them, "but I see the good you are doing, and I want to give you my savings to continue the work."[7] Eleven years later, they had twenty-five cities flourishing with student movements.

With a degree in theology under his belt, Iman sensed from

the Lord that he needed to study Islam and politics. "If God said you should study counseling or discipleship, that would make sense. That's what I would pick, as I was the leader of a big student movement discipling people, studying in small groups, and giving guidance to young people. But Islam and politics?"[8] Still, Iman knew that God was leading him toward this course of study.

In consistent times of prayer, God impressed on the Santosos that they'd need to set aside five years for study and that they'd be going to the United States. Only one interdenominational seminary in America offered a PhD in Islam, so the Santosos followed the Lord's specific instructions to sell their house and prepared their hearts to move to Pasadena, California, to begin studies at Fuller Theological Seminary.

On the ground at Fuller, Lea turned to the Lord one day and sensed a clear word: "Tomorrow, two men will come—one older, one younger. They will offer Iman a position in ministry. He must say no." She sensed that the even though Iman loved people more than books, the Lord wanted Iman to focus all his efforts on his studies, to be an A student.[9]

The next day, just like Lea had expected, two pastors, one older and one younger, came to ask the Santosos to lead a local Indonesian church. When the Santosos declined, the pastors became frustrated, having come with certainty that Iman and Lea would say yes. But God's directions were clear: No ministry. Only studying. All As.

As he entered the circle of the other doctoral students whose mother tongue was English, Iman had to work harder translating his research and writing from his native language. He did his best, day and night thinking only of his studies, but at times, he found his work to be subpar. Still, the Lord assured him and urged him to press on. Iman knew that God never said it would be easy, but only that he had to do it, and that He would be with him through it all.

Even when nine out of ten professors rejected Iman's proposal to study the religious tensions that surfaced during the formation of the Indonesian constitution, Iman sensed the Lord's approval. He had to gather primary sources from Indonesia, something that felt almost impossible from his location in the States, yet he pressed on and faced each issue as it came.

In the five-year time frame set aside for Iman's studies at Fuller, he ended up completing two doctorates exploring the relationship between Islam and the state in Indonesia, researching resources from Muslim scholars. His dissertation covered the Islamization of Iran, Turkey, and all of the Middle East, and considered the signs that there could be an Islamist agenda in his country. With God as Iman's mentor, at the end of his studies at Fuller, he received a transcript covered with nothing but As.

As the Santosos ended their time at Fuller, Lea received further directions from the Lord: "After this, you will go back to Jakarta for a short time. Then, I will bring you to Harvard University."[10] *Harvard?* they questioned. Studying further at a school like Harvard had not even been on the Santosos' radar. Yet they knew where God was leading them. Pressing on through many challenges and getting all As had all worked for a purpose—to carry Iman to the next phase of study. Now they knew without a doubt that God must have a specific reason for them to go to Harvard, too.

The education Iman received, both at Fuller and Harvard, gave him the knowledge he needed to move forward in the next steps of ministry. Because of the insights gained researching and writing, Iman can now analyze a situation through the filter of the Muslim perspective, allowing him to work alongside his diverse Indonesian countrymen with a heart of friendship and diplomacy. The degrees on his resume have also earned him respect and opened up positions of influence in his home country. God didn't want Iman to go to Harvard because *God* is impressed by Ivy League degrees. No, God wanted Iman to go to Harvard because *people* are. God was preparing Iman to minister in high-level circles where accolades matter. Through following God's every prompting, Iman has earned the authority to speak into the everyday moments and historical moves of his nation. God has given him a platform from which to be heard.

A NEW LENS

Whatever the physical or spiritual landscape around us looks like, God wants us to pray and allow Him to comfort us, counsel us, and give us a vision for the situations around us. He wants us to pray because our ministry is more than tasks and to-do lists. He wants us to pray so that our work flows from our relationship with the tender, nurturing God whose will is to redeem all creation.

When my friend Steve Weber moved to Ukraine after the fall of the Iron Curtain, he often found himself overwhelmed with the sad state of the orphan crisis there. Though orphan care has long been a major institution in the former Soviet Union, the emphasis has been more on "orphan" and less on "care."

Over the years, through the camera lens and microphone in his ministry with Christian Broadcasting Network, Steve has been hard at work telling the story of this segment of the population that is overlooked and abandoned. Behind the scenes, Steve and his small circle of friends have felt an intense burden for righting this wrong and have committed to bringing orphans into their own loving families. Steve and his wife adopted for the first time in 1995. But with all of the prejudice against orphans in Ukrainian culture, even in the Ukrainian church, Steve wondered how the Lord might spread the spirit of adoption beyond the small circle of caring souls that they knew.

Steve and his wife encouraged people to adopt. They celebrated all the humanitarian aid being given to orphans. They talked with adoptive parents and Christian orphanages about gathering and doing something bigger, yet they couldn't get traction. One day in 2008, Steve invited a group over to pray in his living room. He looked his friends in the eyes and said, "Guys, what we do right now could be the most important thing we do today, so let's pray and not quit until we hear from God."[11]

Steve recalls there was a feeling of electricity among them, that they could sense God's nearness. It was during that meeting, during intense prayer, that Nikolai Kuleba spoke his heartache aloud to God in one sentence: "Lord, I want to live in a Ukraine without orphans."[12]

Steve says, "Most everything we do, we do as if we're seeing through a glass darkly, but when Nikolai spoke that prayer aloud, it was as if a light came on."[13] Nikolai had captured God's heart in those words. "People get around the table to try to come up with a name for their organization," Steve continues. "They come up with vision statements. They come up with mission statements. 'Let's use this word or that.' But all of a sudden, we had God's vision, mission, and calling in three simple words: Ukraine Without Orphans. It was audacious. It was beyond all of us. But we knew for certain this was what God wanted us to go for."[14]

PRAYER VERSUS PROMOTION

At that point, the group of friends began to meet regularly to put some legs on the calling. About ten years ago, when I learned of the work Steve and his friends were doing, how they were mobilizing each church to commit to adopting a certain number of children and thereby starting to clean out the local foster system, I was fascinated. I sensed, as they did, that this strategy had been handed to them straight from the Lord and that this incredible vision was meant to go beyond Ukraine. God was stirring in our hearts a yearning for a world without orphans. That small prayer meeting in 2008 prepared the way for a worldwide phenomenon that God is using to place the lonely in families today.

In the course of just a few years, Ukraine Without Orphans spawned Russia Without Orphans and Belarus Without Orphans. An orphan care group in Romania called to say they wanted to change the name of their organization to Romania Without Orphans. A Transform World Summit participant from Uganda said that through this movement, on one single Sunday, all forty orphans in their village were adopted by his fellow church members. Now our friend has a vision to see this in every village in his nation. He is looking ahead to Uganda Without Orphans.

Steve says, "No snowflake in an avalanche thinks the result is its fault. We all heard from the Holy Spirit and it just started to snowball. If man tries to promote, we have to use all the marketing techniques and we have to go down this path and go down that path. But when the Holy Spirit starts to do something, He gets it into the right people's hands with or without you."[15]

In Ukraine, the "right hands" have been not only those of the evangelical church, but also those of the Orthodox Church, a very hierarchical structure that feeds out into every single parish of the country. In 2012, Ukraine Without Orphans put out their information on the National Day of Prayer for Orphans. Little did they know that this information would land itself in the office of the Ukrainian Orthodox Church. Soon, the church called and asked for permission to extend this call to prayer to each of their approximately eight thousand parishes. The Roman Catholics did the same. Then, in November 2014, both branches of the Ukrainian Orthodox Church, along with several Catholic churches, and all the evangelical branches gathered on one stage in unity to pray for orphans. Imagine what could happen if each of the churches or parishes in the nation would come forth with one family committed to at least one adoption. Imagine the ripple effect, the yes effect. "The church could close the foster system," Steve says. "It's the only institution that could."[16]

In prayer, Steve and his friends tuned in to the grand plan that the Lord had in mind. In prayer, the Holy Spirit affirmed their desire to help a people, and He gave them a new approach. As a result of prayer, the group came away with specific orders for where to go, what to tackle, precisely how to go about it, and who to team up with.

As I see it, prayer is the most effective and least expensive way to do ministry. We could waste years sitting in rooms, surrounded by walls, developing man-made strategies, refining our mission statements with our teams, or staying back behind closed doors with no clear direction. But there are people wallowing in poverty of both body and spirit, waiting on someone to help them find a better trajectory. Before we can know where to go and what to do, we need to prepare in prayer.

PRAYING THROUGH THE WINDOW

In prayer, we learn that God has people ready to help us in the place that draws our hearts yet overwhelms our senses. As we connect with the Lord in prayer, we learn that there is more to a crisis than meets the eye, that even the most incorrigible people and problems can be redeemed. God wants us to come to Him to make bold requests and bold moves.

The statistics and mapping software I used in 1989 made the vision for the desperate, sprawling area of the 10/40 Window a lot clearer. But I knew we could expect to see nothing of great value and longevity if we weren't devoted to closing our eyes in prayer, to fixing our eyes on Jesus, the author and perfecter of our faith (Heb. 12:2). I told my friend Peter Wagner, coordinator of the AD2000 Prayer Mobilization Network, that we had to recruit a vast number of strategic prayer partners saying, "Lord, give me the 10/40 Window, or I'll die." It sounds dramatic, but that's how intense it felt to us. We were deep into the fray for those who didn't know Jesus and His redemptive work. Our hearts felt so tied to this vision that we weren't satisfied with just going to the Lord on our own, as a small group of mission strategists. We wanted believers all over the world to join us and lean into God together, praying for breakthrough. We hoped for at least a million intercessors. To our amazement, we got many times that amount. If you were involved in an evangelical church in the 1990s, you or your parents may well have been one of those intercessors.

With the help of *Praying through the Window* pamphlets distributed in 1993, churches worldwide prayed for 62 nations of the 10/40 Window. As it turned out, God exceeded my vision by involving 105 nations with over 21 million believers from 28,107 churches and 569 ministries.

While most prayed in their homes or churches, there were also "a reported 607 prayer journeys that originated from 48 different nations."[17] In 1995, nearly 37 million believers prayed for one hundred gateway cities from West Africa to East Asia, which my friend Peter Wagner described as having only a tiny Christian minority and being "the strategic cultural, religious or political centers which influence the spiritual condition of an entire region."[18]

While people prayed, Doris and I were able to take part in a team that visited Calcutta, India (officially renamed Kolkata in 2001), one of those gateway cities. There we walked the crowded streets among the six million inhabitants of the city's 3,000 slum areas. As thousands of villagers migrated to the city from the countryside, hoping for a better life, they would find only squalor. Whole families lived in a space smaller than an average American minivan. The most fortunate shared a single toilet among fifty people. Few enjoyed the luxury of electricity. Another 200,000 people didn't have a home at all. We marveled at the flood of humanity crossing the most congested bridge in the world with six lanes of buses, streetcars, human-powered rickshaws, bicycles, and herds of buffalo, goats, and sacred cows.

There is no better way to know how to pray than to enter a place, walk the streets, listen to the language, and sense the citizens' hopes for their homeland. After coming face to face with the overwhelming need of Calcutta, Doris and I and so many others who had set foot in the gateway cities of the 10/40 Window had much information to pass along to our prayer partners.

As part of our ongoing prayer initiatives for those gateway cities, millions of Christians across the world joined in concerted prayer for Calcutta on October 18, 1995. And in Calcutta itself, Christians from 160 churches met for "eight prayer concerts, and participated in other prayer seminars and prayer walks to claim the city for Jesus Christ."[19] A continuing local prayer initiative in Calcutta "aimed to establish a church in each of the city's 93 postal code zones within three years. When the network was launched, 65 of the zones had no Christian witness. Within two years, 35 zones had ministries established out of the 65 unreached zones."[20] All over the world and in the gateway cities themselves, the church was closing its eyes to the world, and fixing them on Jesus.

In 1997, one American church, Bethany World Prayer Center of Baton Rouge, Louisiana, published prayer profiles of Joshua Project's 1,739 priority unreached people groups of the 10/40 Window, allowing prayer partners to come before the Lord with very specific requests for His will to be done on earth as it is in heaven. Rick Wood of Missions Frontiers reported that without the aid of today's social media marketing, the effort involved "two years of development, over 50,000 man hours, over 40 ministries participating together, [and] over $450,000 invested in research and printing."[21] But this investment prepared the way for rejuvenation among these peoples, providing information for very specific prayers to push back against the kingdom of darkness in the most hard-hit areas of the world.

LATITUDE AND LONGEVITY

In January 2001, our AD2000 Movement closed its doors as we had long planned it would do at the turn of the millennium. It was a strange feeling to realize that for the first time in thirty years, I had no specific ministry task before me. As we moved into a new house, my son asked if I could share a selection of Scripture the next morning. In prayer that night, I asked the Lord what He would have me focus on, not only for the morning devotions, but for my next steps. As I rested in bed, the scene of Jacob's ladder began to play through my mind. "How awesome is this place!" I whispered, echoing Jacob's thoughts in Genesis 28. Whether I was dreaming in sleep or experiencing a vision, I sensed the presence of God palpably as I saw angels going up and down this ladder connecting heaven and earth. In some ways, I could see that ladder resembling the rungs of latitude in our area of focus, the 10/40 Window. In that holy moment, the Lord impressed on me the importance of spreading out to the west, east, north, and south. We had begun with the 10/40 Window, and now I could see that the model of transformation in the most difficult areas of ministry could be transplanted to other impoverished areas of the world outside those latitudes.

The Lord also laid on my heart a passion for transferring this vision of transformation not only to my own descendants, but to children all over the globe. The specifics would play out over time as I began to step out and take action, but that night, out of a dream in the dark, God gave me a vision for what I was to do next.

HOUSES MADE OF PRAYER

As it turns out, my current role as a catalyst for the grassroots movement Transform World was itself born out of a prayer initiative. When the Santosos moved back to Indonesia in the 1990s, the Lord led them to develop a national prayer movement connecting forty mission groups and more than five hundred cities through various networks for pastors, women, and youth. "Everybody gains when we are connecting, when we are in unity," Iman says.[22] Building on their twenty-five years of networking ministry in Indonesia, in 2005 Iman and Lea utilized the administrative gifting of our friend Djohan Handoyo and coordinated to fill up an entire stadium for a prayer rally. Around the same time, Iman, Lea, Djohan, and other brothers and sisters from developing countries came to me saying they wanted to team up to work toward transformation, both spiritual and physical, in their own corners of the globe. This trend has grown in recent decades as the Lord has been springing up indigenous movements all over the world, led not by missionaries from the West, but by the nationals in each country.

There in that stadium as an estimated 80,000 of us prayed together, we christened the vision for Transform World by hosting the largest prayer meeting ever held in Indonesia to that date. Countless others connected via satellite from other cities. Seven years later, the Indonesians did it again, as more Indonesians came to pray in Jakarta National Stadium, with Christians in 378 other cities connecting from their homes and churches via satellite television.

This commitment to prayer continues as organizations team up under the Transform World movement. One of our focus areas in the movement today is building and connecting houses of prayer to encourage worship of our Lord and intercession for ministry around the globe. In our years of establishing houses of prayer, my friends Fred and Sue Rowe and I have noticed that if complacency, or stunted faith, rules in a Christian community, it can be as difficult to build and sustain a house of prayer as it is in areas where there are very few Christians. Yet small numbers in unified agreement with God can move mountains and shift atmospheres, transforming entire communities.[23] If we want to witness that kind of change, it is vital that we turn our eyes toward Jesus to see as He sees.

ALREADY WORKING

What is it that ignites your heart but also ignites your anxiety? What people, place, or problem in front of you feels too big or daunting to touch? What global or local issues have charged you up or gotten you down? Race issues? The worldwide refugee crisis? Human trafficking? Broken families? Start by taking a few minutes of uninterrupted time to pray through that news story or that troubling text from a friend. Admit your worry and heaviness to the Lord. Acknowledge God's presence and power in and above it all. Ask the Lord where He is already at work in the situation and how He wants to work in and through you as you walk through the situation with Him. Pay attention to any verses, thoughts, or images He brings to your mind. Write them down as mementos of your time in prayer. Listen for invitations to engage the situation that overwhelms you. Then, answer the Lord with an affirmative, committing to act on whatever tangible opportunity He opens up for you.

Even if we have begun to feel a burden for the needs of the world and sense the heart of God for the hurting and broken, we must be vigilant not to allow overwhelming feelings or worry to paralyze us. In 2 Corinthians 4:16 and 18, Paul encourages us not to lose heart when we see troubles all around. He says we should "fix our eyes not on what is seen, but on what is unseen, since what is seen is temporary, but what is unseen is eternal" (NIV). I urge you to carve out a few minutes a day, a solid hour at least once a week, a longer stretch of a few hours every month or season, and a day or two for retreat every season or year to pray about the needs that burden you.

Imagine what could happen if we imitated the prayer practices of so many faithful followers of Jesus in history and in other parts of the world. Imagine what could happen if we opened our sanctuaries for daily prayer or set up twenty-four-hour houses of prayer in every major city and town in our nation. Imagine if we became more overwhelmed by the presence of God than by the worries of the world.

Whether we close our eyes in solitude or in a circle of believers, whether we approach God spontaneously or in coordinated meetings, prayer allows us to hand over our uncertainties to

God and become open to His vision for a place and a people. In prayer, we team up with God and discover His strategies for bringing fullness where there is hunger, wholeness where there is sickness, beauty where there is destruction, and peace where there is violence. We must close our eyes to what overwhelms us, fix our eyes on Jesus, and prepare to step by faith toward what we cannot yet see. Will you say yes and fix your eyes on Him?

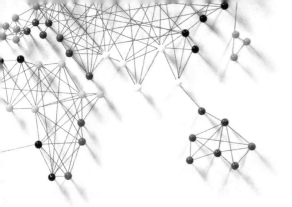

Move Your Feet

As the bus driver pulled the lever to seal the door shut, my friend Ibrahim Haddad and a few of his fellow passengers lamented that they hadn't thought to pick up a bottle of water as they raced to catch their ride. The team had rushed through the sweltering streets of Geneva to make it to the buses for our drive to France where we would be for the remainder of our Transform World 2020 Global Leadership Summit in 2014. Onboard, a cool rush from the air conditioning served as a refreshing prize. Soon, Ibrahim and friends were rolling along the highway, gazing at the beauty of the lush French countryside from the comfort of their chartered bus seats.

But then, a strange sound came from the dashboard of the bus, the sound of sprockets and gears whirring to a stop. The wheels on the bus continued to propel them forward. The engine was still working, but with the sudden thud from the console came a quick interruption to the passengers' comfort. Air was no longer flowing through the vents. Almost immediately, the 90 degree outdoor temperatures and the heat of the engine began to bake the interior of the bus. Riders' cheeks turned a warm shade of red. The fabric on the seats soaked up sweat. It became difficult to get a full breath of oxygen. Passengers began to check on the elderly participants and young children sitting near. As those onboard worked to find some air, the agitation brought on by their discomfort only increased the temperature level. One friend spoke to the driver in French and fiddled with the controls at the front of the bus. Others looked at the large windows and sighed at the fact that there was no way to open them. Ibrahim looked up at the ceiling, at the escape hatch screwed shut. He and a friend did what they could to pry it open, then stuck an orange in as a placeholder to create a small trickle of airflow. One of our house of prayer advocates began to pray aloud for an answer to the problem. As the conditions continued to worsen, the passengers consulted with the driver and decided to pull into a rest stop so everyone could get out of the bus, sip some water from a drinking fountain, and cool down.

As Ibrahim, a brawny fellow much affected by the heat, left the bus, he did so not only without complaining about the sweat on his skin or the change of plans, but also with a sense of expectancy. He trusted the Lord and ascribed to what C. S. Lewis wrote in *The Four Loves*, "But, for a Christian, there are, strictly speaking, no chances. A secret master of ceremonies has been at work."[1]

Ibrahim came out of the restroom, blotting his forehead with a cloth, and soon noticed a truck driver taking a break. This was a man who looked like he might speak Ibrahim's own native language. Ibrahim greeted him in Arabic, the man answered back, and the two talked for nearly thirty minutes while the crew waited for a new bus. In the course of their conversation, Ibrahim handed this Muslim refugee a New Testament, and the two talked about Isa, Jesus. An hour later, when Ibrahim boarded the replacement bus with working air conditioning, he walked up the steps with excitement, explaining to all onboard that their plans for a smooth ride had been thwarted for a reason. Ibrahim trusted that God sometimes allows unpleasant situations so we will step out for the divine appointments He has prepared for us. God gets us uncomfortable to get us moving.

Discomfort can turn our lives upside down, but that doesn't have to be a bad thing. The question is what you will do with it. When your plans are overturned, will you accept God's invitation to turn over your life to Him? Saying yes to a chain-reaction life with God often starts with letting go of our previous plans. World changers cast aside business as usual to take on a higher calling.

FEELING HOMELESS

My friend Raineer Chu grew up running through the Manila slums even though he didn't have to. His father, a middle-class businessman, was often away on work trips, so Raineer was on a long leash, so to speak. With this freedom, he ventured out of his neighborhood and spent his afternoons in the almost-foreign environment of the Manila City Dump where many of his friends lived.

As a young man from a more well-off family, he imagined he must be the only one of his kind frequenting the slums. Just as in Cairo's Garbage City, homes in the Manila City Dump were either built from scrap sheets of metal or cardboard, or, if they were built from stronger material like cement, were crumbling with no one to fix them. Very few citizens of the neighborhood had running water or electricity.

Later on, as a young adult, Raineer met another middle-class visitor to the slums, a social worker named Corrie Acorda De-Boer who was then ministering among street kids in Metro Manila. Soon, a mutual friend in the area, a missionary engineer from New Zealand, Viv Grigg, saw a pioneering tendency in Raineer, and challenged him to pursue it further. While Viv served among the poor of Manila, and as he grew deeper in his understanding of Jesus' heart, he grew "astounded to find no missionary living in the slums,"[2] as he put it. So he became the first, renting a room in a squatter settlement.

When we consider how Jesus left the glory of heaven to come dwell with us, we discover the true meaning of compassion. As Dutch Catholic priest and author Henri Nouwen wrote,

> It is not a bending towards the underprivileged from a privileged position; it is not a reaching out from on high to those who are less fortunate below; it is not a gesture of sympathy or pity for those who fail to make it in the upward pull. On the contrary, compassion means going directly to those people and places where suffering is most acute and building a home there.[3]

Viv's movement to reach the poorest of the poor involves intentionally living with them, "learning from them, building genuine relationships, participating in their lives and struggles, learning their language and their culture, and working out how Jesus' love can best be shown in their context."[4] Viv challenged

Raineer to consider how Jesus took on our way of life, becoming like us and coming near to us, and showed him how he could be a representative of Jesus' living, breathing love in this time and place by making himself more at home in the slums.

The more time Raineer spent in the slums, the more he wanted to invest himself there. "I think it's very infectious when you're there in the middle of it," Raineer laughs.[5] He has camped out in homes built of cardboard. He and his friends have sometimes slept under a bridge in coastal areas. "But we didn't care where we slept," he says.[6] Raineer, so tired from his work, would fall asleep wherever he laid his head, no matter the conditions. He has tried the slum peoples' staple foods, like PagPag, which in the local language means "shaken." The name describes how those who live near the dumps will dig through the garbage, pull out the remnants of food from the rich part of town, shake them to get the dirt loose, then fry them up and serve them. No wonder Raineer has had his share of illness! After all, he does call the lifestyle "infectious."

Home is where the heart is, we often say. When Raineer went back to his home turf, it didn't feel so much like home anymore. "You can't sleep. You don't like your bed. You don't like your food," he said.[7] And maybe this is what we're afraid of. Maybe we're afraid we'll venture into an alternate life and never really be able to get back into the life we think is ours by birthright.

Raineer and his friends plant five churches or so in the slums every year. There is no salary for this kind of work among people who sell scraps from the garbage to barely make a living. Raineer and Corrie's ministry is animated by a heart that beats like God's, that leaves the glory of one place to walk in the dust of another (see Phil. 2:7–8). Their work is largely funded by what we call "tentmaking," like the apostle Paul's business that funded many of his missionary efforts. As a tax lawyer, Raineer serves clients on the more affluent side of town to support his family and ministry. These days, he lives in the middle, between the tax clients and the slums. As he bounces between the two subcultures, he has noticed a great disparity: "Basically, I think the church separates poor Christians from rich Christians all over the world. The rich Christians cannot see the poor Christians."[8] And so, every year, Raineer extends an invitation like Viv Grigg once extended to him, asking ten families or individuals from the wealthy parts of town to join them in planting churches in the slums. Together, they work in the slums and share their resources. In the twenty years of using this model, they have paid their rent without fail for all the venues where the various slum churches meet.

While Raineer was naturally drawn to the mystique of the slums, his wife Mila's story is different. As she put it, "On my own, I probably wouldn't be doing work among the urban poor, honestly."[9] When Raineer was courting her, they always had a sidekick, at least one street kid along for the fun. "That was our date. He would bring me to where the street kids were and, because I'm trained as a medical doctor, I would do some medical checkups and we would give the children a bath."[10] She served, but reluctantly.

Her mother's family had come from among the urban poor. She saw this underprivileged life as something from which to rise up, something to leave behind and not walk back into. She had seen poverty in her family's past and didn't want to see it in her future. Additionally, Mila's introversion makes it difficult for her to entertain crowds. Growing up, her home was a hub for travelers, family, and friends in need of a place to stay in Manila. Mila had trouble with the crowded quarters and lack of privacy and vowed that if she ever had a house of her own, it would be a quiet place kept all to herself. But falling in love with Raineer has required her to relinquish that vision for her life.

She says, "When Raineer went to the urban poor ministry as a full-time worker, it gave me a migraine. It's not like you go to the urban poor and then you go back to your pretty, comfortable house. If you work with the poor, you have the poor with you most of the time. A lot of people come to the house—people who are sick, people who need some legal advice."[11] Today, Mila feels more drawn to the work and the people than she ever thought she would, yet her reserved personality and her knowledge of medical dangers make her more careful than her husband. When Raineer comes home from working at the dump, she stops him at the door, tells him to toss his clothes in the wash, to immediately scrub himself in the bath, and not to get near their kids until he's clean. I think we often picture those living a life of service as having to exhibit the all-in, gung-ho attitude of Raineer. But Mila's example shows us that God can use even a hesitant yes to effect transformation.

Today, Raineer leads a thriving monastic evangelical community called Companion with the Poor, where members value community, incarnational mission, a simple lifestyle, and following Jesus among the poor. It is a sister organization of Mission Ministries Philippines, a grassroots social movement advocating for quality early childhood Christian education among the poor, founded by Corrie, whom Raineer met in the slums, and her husband, Stewart. In partnership with Viv Grigg and his visionary leadership, both Raineer and Corrie are now training a new generation of urban leaders by creating a master of arts program in transformational leadership that will equip leaders to make Jesus known by living and working among the poor. They are also training doctoral candidates of Bakke Graduate University in Texas and the Ray Bakke Centre for Urban Transformation in Hong Kong to engage in this same lifestyle of incarnational ministry.

When we read the stories of people doing unconventional ministry, leaving their comfortable situations to reach others, we can often think they're simply wired differently, that they're natural thrill seekers or adrenaline junkies with an extra dose of something special. We may want some of the adventure and the transformation they're experiencing, but we don't think we have what it takes to get there. The truth is any of us can get out of our status quo existence and become fully alive and fully engaged with our surroundings. It simply requires a yes, whether hearty or timid. Each story takes on its own trajectory depending on the unique personalities and settings that God puts together.

ABOVE GROUND

Stepping out to serve doesn't necessarily mean stepping from a privileged lifestyle into physical poverty. The invitation to be involved in God's chain reaction is different for each person. Indeed, there are needs in all segments of society, including those that don't appear quite as poor on the exterior. Sometimes saying yes is following God to a different kind of unreached people who might not know how needy they truly are. So it was for my friend Ezra Jin. As Ezra, his wife, Anna, and two of their children lived with us in our home in Chicago for eight months a few years ago, we learned so much about what it truly means for a Chinese believer to step out in faith.

Becoming a believer in Jesus as a Chinese citizen had in itself been an act of stepping out for Ezra. By claiming Christ in the spiritual and political environment of his era, he stepped out from the safety and security of being an anonymous part of the masses in his communist country to becoming somewhat of a misfit. Just after the terrible tragedy at Tiananmen Square in 1989, when students leading a democratic protest were gunned down and pushed back by tanks, Ezra came to Beijing to remember a friend who had lost her life in the attack. At the funeral of this young Christian woman, Ezra listened to followers of Jesus sing hymns and share from Luke 15, the story of the prodigal son.

"I never think I am a lost people," Ezra said. "I had attended church several times but I could hardly make sense of the message. I never really thought of God. But suddenly at this funeral, I recognized I might be one of the lost people. I wondered, 'Why do these friends have such strong faith? Why don't I have such hope?'"[12] Ezra didn't know what else to do but to attend church again. And the only option he knew was the Three-Self Church, a state-sanctioned, highly controlled institution, and one of the very few denominations that China has allowed Christians to attend legally.

There at the Three-Self Church, Ezra befriended a student from UC Berkeley. After a few weeks of knowing each other, that student turned to Ezra and asked him if he wanted to become a Christian. "I was surprised," Ezra said. "How did he know I wasn't a real Christian already?"[13] This friend told him that attending worship and Sunday Bible study can never make you a Christian, and then shared the words of Revelation 3:20. Just like Doris and I so many years earlier, Ezra felt Jesus knocking on the door. He was moved. He got down on the floor and prayed for the first time ever. "I don't know if you are real, God," he said. "If You are, then You know me. Please tell me what to do."[14]

He rode his bicycle home from there, trying to focus on the road through his tears, an expressive emotion not often seen in public in China. "I was so happy. I cry. I sing. I really experienced that God is good, that life is good. I experienced comfort so strong. That night, I knew what I needed to do with my whole life, to love God more than anything else."[15] In opening the door of his heart, Ezra invited Jesus in, and then Jesus invited Ezra out to serve, to bring this depth of emotion and this new understanding of God's purposes to people who were like him, people who didn't know they were lost.

For ten years, Ezra served faithfully in the Three-Self Church where he had first become a believer. But Ezra's desire to love God more than anything else was often difficult with the tight control of the state-sanctioned church. The Three-Self movement had been established in the late 1800s by international missionaries to encourage Chinese nationals to take up the leadership of the church and spread the message of Jesus to their own people. A common value in missional philosophy in that era, the "three selfs" (self-govern, self-support, self-propagate) worked with the financial constraints of international mission organizations and sat well with the Chinese who tended to fear foreign leadership, equating it with imperialism. But then during the Cultural Revolution in the late 1960s and early 1970s as Jason Mandryk reports in *Operation World*, all religious institutions including the Three-Self Church were banned and "forced underground." This decision would change the course of history for the church in China. The government's efforts to squelch the church instead gave birth to the house-church movement and thus made the church flourish. Mandryk says that when the government allowed the Three-Self Church to re-emerge in 1978, it did so as a means to gain control of the house-church movement that was spreading like wildfire underground without government oversight.[16]

While Ezra loved the slow-paced elderly men and women who made up the congregation of the Three-Self Church he pastored, he kept feeling a tug from God to go to the lost people in the hub of society and tell them the good news that had brought him to his knees after Tiananmen. Ezra had become a Christian when he saw himself as a lost person part of a lost people. He could not look around at the swarming streets without feeling the same about these city people going about their daily business. The people of Beijing, and of China as a whole, needed to know they were lost.

For Ezra, sharing that message from inside the walls of the Three-Self Church felt like preaching in a soundproof room. "There was some ministry and work we could do in the Three-Self Church, but when the government wants to control, they can do anything they want. They can decide who goes to seminary, who is ordained, what ministry can be done. They can even choose church members," Ezra says.[17] It was at this mental crossroads that Ezra decided to pursue a seminary degree. As a result of his decision, Ezra and I met at Fuller Seminary in 2002. When Ezra returned to China after his studies in the United States, he took a big risk. Ezra's wife and ministry partner, Anna, said, "As soon as he came back in town, everybody knew."[18] The couple was too well-connected in the city to start an underground ministry. Because of his previous work in the Three-Self Church, Ezra was well-acquainted with government officials and could not maintain a low profile even if he tried. His choice was either to go back to pastoring a Three-Self church or to establish a new ministry completely out in the open, lest his government official friends start suspecting he was hiding something. What motivated him was a concern for the spiritual health of his country and a burning desire to share hope with a different kind of unreached people, a tired people whose striving for success was killing them.

In a nation where college students jump from dorm room windows at exam time, where a factory that makes smartphones and computers for tech companies had to install safety nets around the perimeter of the building after ten workers jumped to their deaths in a period of less than six months, there is clearly a need that is not being addressed.[19] Approximately a quarter of a million people commit suicide every year in China, with suicide as the leading cause of death of people between the ages of fifteen and thirty-four.[20]

Ezra tells, "Most people in China have too much pressure, tragedy, and suffering. Nobody comforts them. God wants to do something, and I want to help. I want to comfort these miserable people."[21] With those tired, miserable people in mind, he started a new church above ground, in the hub of society. Having just written his dissertation on the Back to Jerusalem movement—a group of Chinese believers who sought to bring the Great Commission full circle and carry the message of Jesus to every unreached people group along the ancient trade routes between China and the Middle East—Ezra honored the legacy of these brave believers in China's history and named his new ministry Zion Church, Zion being another name for Jerusalem. With a small, bold group of twenty Chinese believers, Ezra and Anna opened the doors of the church in Beijing, not even knowing how they would fund themselves. To their surprise, people streamed in. Young people, lawyers, business professionals—visitor after visitor embraced the message of Jesus and became family in the faith.

Once, in the middle of a church service, a young man with a master's degree from an Ivy League school began to cry. He gave his life to Christ and immediately began to share his faith with his peers. This was different than the stagnant church Ezra had pastored under the thumb of the government. "I was surprised," Ezra said. "The new believers were more ready for training. They were ready to follow."[22]

Since its start in 2007, Zion's congregation has grown both in commitment and size. With up to two thousand people attending services weekly, Zion Church is now the largest in Beijing, like a city on a hill that cannot be hidden. Remarkably, the government has, up to this point, not placed sanctions on Zion Church or its leaders. Whether it's Ezra's soft-spoken approach or God's timing for China, or a combination of the two, the church continues to flourish. "Some say, 'Pastor Jin have some strong background.' I say, 'Yes. We have some strong background. Our heavenly Father is our strong background.' I believe God wants to do a new thing in China," Ezra affirmed.[23]

The relatively easy entrance into new ministry for Ezra has been somewhat surprising. Friends who have gone before him in pastoring house churches have suffered greatly for being outspoken about their faith in a nation that has historically seen religion as a threat to society. Yet, as Jason Mandryk points out, "Further persecutions seemed to only encourage further growth, despite horrendous cruelties inflicted on many thousands of church leaders."[24] Ezra has witnessed firsthand how the Holy Spirit has ministered to a pastor friend who was put on house arrest for three years because of his bold faith, and how the church flourishes even in the midst of efforts to stunt its growth. While the government at times seems to fear possible political action or opposition from Jesus followers in China, only Christians can lead the way to what China needs most.

After the death of Yue Yue, even the Communist Party leader in Guangdong province, Wang Yang, said in an interview, "We should look into the ugliness in ourselves with a dagger of conscience and bite the soul-searching bullet."[25] USA Today reported that "China's ruling party appears to be falling back on traditional, top-down methods to raise moral standards" through state-sponsored morality-building television shows, model-worker awards, and neighborhood citizenship initiatives.[26] China is looking for a new way of life, a new way to help people flourish, and it is for this reason that Ezra believes his ministry will continue to be well-received.

Up to this point, Zion Church remains unregistered and free from the tether of bureaucratic micromanaging. In the attitude of the prophet Daniel, who prayed courageously and peacefully on his windowsill, Ezra chooses to share his ministry openly with government officials. In his view, the government doesn't need to fear the church, nor the church the government. "We don't need to hide. We do good work for China. I want to share everything. God's work in this church has begun a new movement in China as churches emerge positively in society."[27]

When Ezra steps out, he does so not in defiance of the Chinese government, but in defiance of the claims that spiritual darkness has made on his beloved country. He does so in defiance of his fellow citizens' materialism, greed, hard-heartedness, and anything else that opposes the knowledge of Jesus (see 2 Cor. 10:5). When he steps out, it is to push back the kingdom of hell and make way for the kingdom of God. And where God's kingdom is, communities thrive. In Galatians 5:22–23, the apostle Paul spoke right to the heart of the nations who fear, and therefore persecute, the church. The fruit of the Spirit brings about all kinds of beautiful attributes against which "there is no law." Chinese believers in Ezra's church are living examples of the love, joy, peace, patience, kindness, goodness, gentleness, and self-control that even Chinese government officials long to see.

REFUSE AND REFUGE

Stepping out doesn't have to mean stepping into a different socioeconomic class. Neither does it have to mean crossing national borders or oceans. Sometimes moving our feet in sync with the Holy Spirit means stepping out to welcome others who have shown up in our own neighborhoods. And perhaps no other area of the world has welcomed more newcomers in recent days than those Middle Eastern countries receiving Syrians and Iraqis who have fled their war-ravaged nations. For my friend Nabil Salib, stepping out means driving the roads of his country in search of unregistered refugees, those who aren't listed to receive aid from the United Nations. Nabil estimates that only 10 percent of refugees in his nation are actually registered.[28] In January 2016, Doctors without Borders reported, "An astonishing 7.6 million Syrians have been internally displaced, with an additional 4.1 million having fled to Egypt, Iraq, Jordan, Lebanon, and Turkey—the countries bearing the brunt of the refugee crisis—since the start of Syria's civil war in 2011. Combined, this is more than half of the country's 23 million people."[29] A refugee woman with a scar like a giant zipper across her neck, a family with a bombed-out apartment and missing relatives, a toddler in the water—people like these call us to step out and do something.

The refugee crisis became a hot-button topic in the United States in late 2015 as terrorist attacks in Paris, and then an attack in San Bernardino, California, raised questions about the process for vetting those, especially refugees, seeking residency in the United States. In times like this, citizens in more stable countries can be tempted not only to stay inside the safety of their well-tended communities, but even to build higher walls, seeking to protect residents from those who are "other."

This is not a simple issue. The fear that many citizens have expressed should not be dismissed without consideration. As Paul points out in 1 Timothy 2:1–3, we should pray so that we can "lead a peaceful and quiet life, godly and dignified in every way. This is good, and it is pleasing in the sight of God our Savior." No matter our political affiliation, we should pray for our leaders to be wise in cultivating and protecting this place of relative peace, both for ourselves and the weary ones we welcome. What a tragedy it would be to allow in the very terrorists that refugees now in our midst had once escaped, to allow this place of intended safety to become the war zone so many have fled. At the same time, we must work to avoid the tragedy of closing our hearts to those hurled from their homelands into the mountains and seas, those who are searching for the same peaceful, quiet life for themselves. The United States has historically been one of the most charitable, hospitable countries in the world. We must find a way to step out and engage with the huddled masses before us now. This crisis, in all its complexity, is an invitation for us to treat the outsider as God has treated us—with love, with compassion, with mercy.

Some of us are called to work in the places closest to the crisis. Others are called to do their part by helping to relocate the world's displaced peoples to new environments where they can flourish, or by working out kinks in the vetting process to ensure that both our land and those war-ravaged innocents entering it are kept safe. Those of us who have not been called to travel beyond our own cities or towns can be ready and waiting, like my friends Nabil Salib and Ibrahim Haddad, to welcome those who have sought peace in our home country. We all are called to step out of our comfort zone to welcome those coming into our communities, those seeking peace and quiet and a way to feed their families.

When we struggle to connect with those suffering as a result of such complicated situations, it helps to remember times of need in our own lives. When have you felt abused, abandoned, overlooked, tired, or hungry? Remembering our own difficulties, even those that seem small or insignificant in comparison, can help us feel for and act on behalf of those experiencing difficulty now. God Himself urges His people to work from a place of empathy. He encourages His people to think back on their own history and treat others as they themselves wanted to be treated: "You shall treat the stranger who sojourns with you as the native among you, and you shall love him as yourself, for you were strangers in the land of Egypt: I am the LORD your God" (Lev. 19:34). Whether we have experienced trauma on a large scale, such as being estranged from our native land or, on a smaller scale, such as being forced out of a group by a bully, all of us know in some way what it's like to be alienated.

In the Middle Eastern country where my friend Nabil has lived his entire life, citizens are overwhelmed with the number of refugees fleeing civil war in Syria. As natives and newcomers compete for resources, animosity can develop. But Nabil and his fellow workers in the gospel have committed to lean on the generous heart of God, which gives them strength to visit refugees and treat them as their own people.

Nabil does not find a phone booth and change into a superhero costume before visiting the refugee camps and villages. He does not enter loudly and boldly, leaping tall buildings in a single bound. He steps out with kindness and curiosity, knowing God has called him to interact with these people. He brings a housewarming gift, a box of food and supplies to show each family that someone is thinking of their well-being. He goes in looking for places where God is at work, rather than going in with a ready-made agenda.

Perhaps you can try the same approach where you are. Get in touch with a local organization to learn how to meet the specific needs of refugees. Team up with friends to gather clothing, household supplies, and gift cards to grocery stores. Offer to drive refugees to job interviews, to the store for their weekly shopping, or simply around town to get their bearings in the city. Acknowledge their holidays with greetings or gifts. Find an interpreter to join you, or simply do your best with hand motions and free online translation tools. Teach them useful words and phrases in English and learn some of their language in the process. Or think big and start a whole range of English classes at your church for refugees or other internationals.

Beyond supporting refugees with material goods or helpful services, there is also a need to simply offer your friendship. People need to know they are not marginalized. They need to know that they are not merely tolerated, but are treasured and welcomed. Receive their tears. Let them tell you the hard stories of the decimated cities they left. Your care and attention can provide these people a nurturing place to recover after the trauma they've endured.

You may not have the knowledge or power to ensure the vetting process is either rigorous enough or humane enough, but you can show hospitality and care to the refugees who relocate to your area. Acts 17:26–27 tells us, "He made from one man every nation of mankind to live on all the face of the earth, having determined allotted periods and the boundaries of their dwelling place." Why? "That they should seek God, and perhaps feel their way toward him and find him." The refugee crisis, for the Jesus follower, could actually be called the refugee *opportunity*, an invitation to be brave and kind, to help a weary people feel their way toward God and experience His acceptance and provision.

YOUR TURN

But what about when we feel weary just keeping up with the needs of our own communities or families? If you feel too tired and discouraged to help anyone else, perhaps you need to simply act in the right direction and trust that the energy to keep going will come. Dr. David Stoop writes in his book *You Are What You Think* that the quickest way out of apathy is to plan to do something and then do it. He writes, "Do something, no matter how small a step it is. . . . It is the willful choice to act that breaks through our sense of helplessness. . . . If it is a good thing to do, do it and give yourself permission to enjoy it."[30] Get in motion and motivation will follow.

Our faith is not some ethereal belief system that rests merely in the spiritual realm. Our faith is meant to be active, visible evidence of God's renewing work in the world. Have you ever tried Pop Rocks candy? When they're in the package, they're lifeless and quiet. But when you put them in your mouth, they start crackling and fizzing. Similarly, you have to activate your faith to experience the full energy and flavor of it.

Start moving. Pick the issue that has burdened you and choose one small act to address that need today. Look at the plenty in your life and choose a way to lavish blessings on a weary person. Find someone from a different ethnic background who's willing to talk through cultural tensions. Become a welcome wagon to a newcomer. Walk alongside a struggling family and offer a warm meal or childcare in the middle of their crisis. Be generous and you'll find your own weariness starting to lessen. As Proverbs 11:25 (NIV) tells us, "A generous person will prosper; whoever refreshes others will be refreshed." Act and you will find a new energy to act again.

As Henry Blackaby writes in *Experiencing the Spirit: The Power of Pentecost Every Day*,

> Listen carefully: *Recognizing God* is not the same as coming to Him. *Hearing God* in your heart is not the same as answering. *Working for the kingdom of God* does not mean living in the kingdom of God. Christianity is not believing the truths of the Bible; it's *acting* upon them and allowing God control of your life. You must *respond* to God and make the choice to interact personally with Him.[31]

Your response to God's daily invitations will determine how much of His renewing work in the world you will get to see. Will you step off the bus into fresh air and start a conversation? Will you let go of your concept of a neat and tidy life and not just donate food to those who live in scarcity, but actually eat *with* them? Will you follow Nabil Salib's lead and make the effort to visit the visitors in your community, extending a hand of friendship? Will you start something new, like Ezra Jin and Raineer Chu did, even if it causes people to raise their eyebrows? Whatever it is, it's your turn to do something, to get on your feet and see what happens.

Find Your People

The weathered woman smoothed her headscarf and bent down to the ground, gleaning grain in the field to provide for her five fatherless children. Amira had been widowed by divorce, sent away by a husband who apparently liked her least of his many wives. Though abandoned, she continued to work hard raising her kids to help them reach their potential. The future began to brighten as Amira's oldest daughter completed her nursing degree, which promised a steadier income for the family. But at that pivotal moment, a tragic car accident took the young lady's life. Amira and her other children lost not only their beloved family member, but also their hope for a more secure financial future.

Like Amira and her family, the people we want to help are often already overcoming challenges and working toward their own well-being, using whatever opportunities are in reach. Often they just need a teammate, someone whose gifting, experience, and skills complement theirs, to get them to a more sustainable way of living.

Through periodic visits over the course of several years, my friend Nabil Salib, a native of the Middle East, and his American friend Scott Gillis—who brings in teams from his church in California—have combined their unique personalities, backgrounds, and resources to cultivate relationships in impoverished areas in Nabil's nation. Together, they have listened to Amira's story and her hopes for her kids, observed her commitment to hard work, kept an ear open for her needs, and worked together to find resources for the family. When Nabil's nonprofit organization allowed Amira to borrow a goat to milk and breed, Scott's team helped Amira find a refrigerator to keep the perishable by-products from spoiling. They mentored her in her efforts to provide for her family as she sold some of the milk, yogurt, and cheese to create an income and kept the remainder to nourish her children. And while Nabil and Scott ministered to the family's practical needs, their friendship with the family grew. With repeated visits, the youngest of the children began running up to Nabil and Scott, calling each of them "Uncle." Later, the team celebrated with the family upon hearing news that Amira's second daughter had accepted a scholarship from their ministry to attend nursing school, in remembrance of her sister.

Back in the United States, one of the teenagers from Scott's first team wanted to let Amira's daughter know she, too, was celebrating her friend's move forward. And so she collected enough money to pay the bus fare for the young woman to travel to nursing school. It wasn't a huge expense, but it was specific and touched Amira's daughter's heart. In her second year of nursing school, the young woman gave a presentation at a gathering on a national holiday and spoke about how her life had been changed by meeting a group of Christians. When she graduated from nursing school, she wanted to work someplace where there were Christians, so she sought employment at a mission hospital.

When Nabil's organization was seeking an official certificate for serving in that particular nation, Amira and other people from the village showed up and said, "We love these people. They're doing a good thing in our village."[1] This testimony of successful teamwork with Amira has allowed Nabil's ministry the credibility it needs to partner with other families in the area for the long-term and encourage physical and spiritual wholeness to multiply throughout the community. Through vibrant working relationships with neighbors and with Nabil's team, Amira's family is on the journey to healing and sustainability. Not only that, they have an understanding of God that is growing day by day. Nabil and his teammates say they are providing a pixel here and a pixel there to help fill in the image of what the kingdom of God is like on earth. While the people in these communities may not see the whole picture of God's love just yet, they are starting to get a glimpse.[2]

THE PERSON OF PEACE

If we want to see true transformation in the community we're seeking to help, we need to team up not just with fellow believers, but also with those who don't know Jesus. When my friends and I develop a heart and vision for reaching out to a new community, we prepare through prayer and careful research, but we do not expect to march in and meet the needs of the community based solely on that initial preparation. With a belief in the significance and dignity of all people, we go in slowly, humbly, with a desire to know and learn.

We lean into the "person of peace" model, the way of ministry Jesus Himself outlined in Luke 10:1–9. In one of the largest ministry initiatives during His time on earth, Jesus appointed seventy-two messengers, dividing them into pairs to go "ahead of him, two by two, into every town and place where he himself was about to go" (v. 1). As they went, they were to focus not on meeting their own needs, but on finding locals who would receive them, and ultimately, the message of Jesus. "Whatever house you enter, first say, 'Peace be to this house,'" Jesus said. "If a son of peace is there, your peace will rest upon him. But if not, it will return to you. And remain in the same house, eating and drinking what they provide, for the laborer deserves his wages. Do not go from house to house. Whenever you enter a town and they receive you, eat what is set before you. Heal the sick in it and say to them, 'The kingdom of God has come near to you'" (vv. 5–9).

A man or woman of peace is someone who is receptive to our visit and can help us tune our senses to the culture, personality, potential, and needs of a community. The person of peace can be either a believer in Jesus or simply someone who has an open mind and heart. As in the case of Amira, the person of peace is willing, even eager, to introduce the visitor to the community and vouch for the visitor's character. The person of peace is compassionate, servant-hearted, and a good listener who meets the needs of both the visitor and the community. When we come as outsiders ready to serve, it is vital that we humble ourselves and accept the leadership of the person of peace in the community so that, with an attitude of respect, we may effectively offer our help to those who need it most.

Scott and Nabil believe strongly in the importance of building an ongoing friendship with a person or family of peace. Scott says, "You'll find where there's a friendly heart like Amira's, the influence will radiate out from that one family to the rest of the village. As you're going, you can relate to the other people in the village. You don't need to fix the whole village yourself. You can't. You're just trying to find where God may have prepared someone's heart. You will become a light to that person, and hopefully that person will become a light to others as well. Then their credibility in telling the story about how you've helped them is far greater than your credibility of saying, 'I helped.'"[3]

I've heard of groups from suburban American churches that have gone into urban neighborhoods with a prepackaged program for the neighborhood children, yet found attendance to be lackluster as families were, for one reason or another, resistant to their presence there. Part of the hesitation may result from tensions between people of differing socioeconomic and cultural backgrounds, but there also may be a simple lack of true partnership, leaving the local families stuck in an "us and them" mentality. When plans and programs are ready-made, there may be very little, if any, ownership on the part of the residents who actually live in the neighborhood. It may be a more time-intensive process at the start, but there is greater hope for longevity of a worthy work if it is built around a team mindset rather than a giver-receiver mindset. It could save a great deal of energy and heartache first to connect with a few of the residents, asking them to shed light on their hopes for their community, what they feel is lacking there, how they feel they are equipped to address the issues, and what role they might picture for their suburban counterparts. If people aren't participating and taking on ownership, their hearts and minds won't be receptive. If hearts and minds aren't receptive, our help may not seem like help at all. It's quite possible that residents of the urban neighborhood could end up thinking the ready-made program is a good idea, but if outsiders come in ready to give answers instead of first asking questions, or focusing more on plans than people, good intentions will likely fall flat before they even get off the ground.

I've also heard of church plants that have gone about building a core membership by reaching their neighborhood in creative, engaging ways that partner the churched and unchurched in mutual work. Instead of, or along with, running ads to attract people to church programs, these churches have gone out to survey their neighbors about the needs of the community. Thoughtful believers start conversations, make connections, and work together to take care of neighbors and the physical spaces of the community. Other churches have cultivated meaningful relationships with residents surrounding the church by passing out small cards with a section for residents to write a request if they'd like to have someone pray with or for them. One church with a food pantry, community garden, and prayer counseling ministry for the poor has had more requests for prayer than for groceries. Food pantry beneficiaries feel so known and loved that they keep coming back to donate staple items and talk about their spiritual needs, even when they're no longer in need of help to stock the fridge at home. Personal connections and partnerships encourage healthy ongoing ministry, whether it be through a formal organization or informal interactions with the people you care about.

The "person of peace" model can be helpful, even vital, in any context that you enter as a newcomer or outsider. There is no better research than the kind that comes through a person who has lived the reality that the statistics reflect. When we go in with a needs-based approach, which focuses on what people lack, we end up with services delivered by outsiders, passive recipients or consumers, and negative mindsets. The healthier approach is an asset-based tactic that focuses on what people have. This results in sustainable development, creates active participants or producers, restores dignity to the people, and builds their confidence. As my friend Terry Dalrymple said, "It is very important to see the people we serve as made in the image of God . . . stewards of resources, not victims of circumstance. Transformational community development workers must look beyond the need."[4] We must look beyond the need of a community and get to know the uniquely gifted people who reside there. In the team-building approach, individuals consider how they are made and then work together to match their talents to the troubles in front of them, saying yes to engaging with the issues in a way that fits who they are. We each play our part while leaving room for others to play theirs, too.

THE WAITING ROOM

When I was a young businessman in Chicago, another businessman, John Warton, tapped me on the shoulder and invited me to a Bible study. Ironically, God would use that Bible study in that high-rise apartment to lead both John and me out of the business world and into church leadership as pastors. Yet while in his pastoral role, John found he wasn't completely done with the business world. Over his fifteen years in the local church context, he found himself asking how businesspeople whom he was shepherding could fulfill the Great Commission in their local community and even overseas. He observed that evangelicals tend to think that businesspeople contribute to the Great Commission mostly by funding the work of pastors, missionaries, and other Christian workers. While giving generously is indeed a vital function of those in the business world, it isn't all that they are good for. John saw something more. He said, "In a society where job creation is often a very high national priority, who is going to do that? Not pastors or missionaries, unless they have been trained in business and have experience in a particular field. Governments aren't very good at job creation. If anything, they tend to hinder business."[5]

The need for job growth worldwide goes beyond the image of malnourished children with distended bellies, or even families living in shacks made of cast-off trash. We may look at those images for a moment, feeling a little sorry for the poor and wishing they had a way up from their rock-bottom. But then we move along in our daily routines unsure what bearing the problems half a world away should really have on our lives. We don't know how to solve the problems, so to feel better, we just put them out of our minds. They're someone else's problems anyway. But you may want to take a second look because that scene of poverty showing up on your newsfeed could end up morphing into something much more frightening, something that can become not just a problem for the poor of the world, but a problem for the world as a whole.

Human rights advocate and Somalian native Mohammed Ali (not the late, great boxer) says in his TED Talk that 70 percent of young people are out of school and out of a job in his home city, and that this "story repeats itself in urban centers around the world . . . the story of the disenfranchised, unemployed, urban youth who sparks riots," even leading to acts of terrorism.[6] In this scenario, sometimes called "waithood," young people are deprived of the opportunity to make a living, and this waiting deprives them of moving forward in their lives—marrying, having children, and making a positive mark on the world. Young people feel like they're in a societal straitjacket. This hopelessness leaves them vulnerable to being recruited by unsavory movements that promise them a future. And Ali believes that for our own safety, good people must do something to help these people feel less closed in and more empowered. Businesspeople have the opportunity to help alleviate some of the worst acts of violence in the world simply through entrepreneurship and job growth. In essence, businesspeople can help other potential businesspeople become the solution to their own problems.

In Luke 19:11–26, Jesus tells us a parable of a man of great influence who endows ten servants with a portion of his wealth. John Warton explains the parable this way:

> They knew that he would come back and that he would expect of them an increase of what he entrusted to them. This is exactly the way men and women in business in every country are looking at their opportunity, the stewardship of their

financial resources, their athletic ability, their artistic skills, their entrepreneurial skills. They see themselves as stewards of these resources and they're looking for the day when the Lord will ask them, "What have you done with what I've given you?" When the wealthy man left the servants each with a coin in hand, he affirmed the importance of business enterprise, "Do business with this money until I get back."[7]

The investor saw potential in each of the recipients and trusted that each individual could and would use the funds to invest in worthy endeavors in order to multiply the money.

Businesspeople have the incredible opportunity to address all sorts of the challenges our communities face. John says business growth creates income that alleviates poverty, provides food for the starving, and makes medicine available to the sick. It provides families the income necessary to bring orphaned children into their homes, allows older orphans without families to find meaningful work and to integrate into society, and creates an environment in which business owners can lift up the poor, both by purchasing from the poor and selling to them, with fair prices at both ends of the deal.[8]

While we want all people to have the opportunity to work, what we ultimately want is for them to come to know Christ— the inspiration behind our work. In Warton's model, the goal is to grow Christian-owned businesses that will bless whole communities in the ways mentioned above, but his Business Professional Network (BPN) also partners with non-Christian "persons of peace" who are open to being mentored by Christian business professionals. Either way, sharing Jesus is the vitality of business missions.

JUMP-START A DREAM

In his book, *Business as Mission: A Comprehensive Guide to Theory and Practice*, business scholar C. Neal Johnson tells the story of traveling with John Warton to my beloved El Salvador, where they visited a baker named Rollo. Due to total deafness, Rollo had previously been unable to find long-term work to sufficiently provide for his family. So with no work accessible to him, he decided to create a job for himself. After presenting a business plan for a wholesale bakery and applying for a loan, Rollo received funds from John's network to purchase a large oven. John says that while microloans can help individuals and families meet their own immediate needs, real business growth occurs with larger loans ranging from $1,000 to $10,000, and even up to $25,000. He believes that small- and medium-sized businesses receiving larger loans are better equipped to create jobs and provide income to help families, churches, communities, and nations. Johnson reports that with the new oven, Rollo was able to make enough bread and rolls on a daily basis to supply local restaurants. In turn, he was able to pursue ways of delivering the bread. He purchased a new fleet of bicycles and invested in another craftsman entrepreneur, a local weaver who would make large baskets to mount between the handlebars. Then Rollo recruited capable young people to deliver his bread for a commission. The business multiplied from there and Rollo was able to repay his loans with funds from his business. Since then, he has built a home for his family on the second story of the bakery and, despite his challenges, has become a productive citizen.[9]

In the same nation, BPN has helped men and women launch

or grow careers as furniture makers, dry goods merchants, electronics repairmen, and motorcycle mechanics. Other BPN endeavors throughout the world include publishing, television production and distribution, management training, computer training, software design, high-tech consulting, engineering, air freight, construction, radio stations, tourist hotels, and other careers.[10] As you can see, there is a wide variety of enterprise, a wide-open invitation for people of all backgrounds to partner in jump-starting the dream of a person in a developing community. John says that the average American businessperson knows enough to put on a weeklong seminar, while our entrepreneur friends overseas have had virtually no training in business.[11]

But this principle works beyond the business realm and beyond developing nations. Businessperson or not, we all have skills, expertise, and resources to share. As I've paired my penchant for inquiry, data, and vision for various issues in the world with Iman Santoso's ceaseless prayer and unifying diplomacy skills, and added that to our friend Djohan Handoyo's gifts of administration and logistics, we have seen a great expansion of unified prayer and localized outreach take place across the world. When we team up with fellow believers and the people in the communities we hope to reach, momentum begins to build and individuals begin to see just who God has designed them to be.

What can you offer to those who need help getting their ideas off the ground? How could you bless other individuals with your unique personality, skills, and experience, and in turn bless an entire community? Teaming up with people like you might just help an entrepreneur grow their company, create jobs, and provide ways for others to step out from the waiting rooms of the world. Transformation is effected more powerfully when we team up with others. Every believer has something vital to contribute.

A SPIRITUAL ECOSYSTEM

Community innovation and personal development does not have to be fancy. Father Sama'an's friends in Garbage City are proof of that. Their heritage goes back to a group of peasant farmers who migrated from Upper Egypt to Cairo in search of new, more viable work in the 1930s and 1940s. These people, Coptic Orthodox Christians by birth, brought their pigs with them and continued to raise them to provide food for them-selves or to sell to tourist hotels in their predominantly non-pork-eating nation. To keep their livestock fed, they began to pay Muslim garbage collectors for food scraps. Soon, in this ongoing interaction, the Christians began hauling and sorting for the city's garbage collectors. Over time, as they took on more of the work, they took on the majority of garbage collect-ing in the city and became known as the Zabbaleen, an Arabic word for *garbage people*.[12]

They settled into their work there, still maintaining a some-what migrant way of life. Moving from neighborhood to neigh-borhood, they lived in temporary structures, trying to avoid run-ins with government officials who weren't happy about having them around. Eventually, around 1970, the governor of Cairo issued a decree that all of the Zabbaleen must move to the outskirts of the city.[13] Maybe it was the stench of the garbage they piled high in front of their abodes. Maybe it was the smell of the pigs. Whatever the issue, the governor pointed them to a hill in Mokattam and told them to go. This is when the Zabbaleen became literal outcasts. Newly homeless, and forced into the valley, they built huts of tin, identical to the pens in which they kept their pigs.

A few years into their exile, God would call my friend Father Sama'an out from Cairo proper to serve the Zabbaleen. "I will give you every place where you set your foot," Father Sama'an sensed the Lord saying to him.[14] So he walked down every street and alley, through every trash-laden thoroughfare. When Father Sama'an came from the hub of society in his clean clothes, the people skittered into the dark of the pigpens to hide from him. But if the people were going to wallow with the pigs, then so was he. As he stepped through the dark, narrow opening of one of the pens, mud squelched and stole his sandals right off his feet. Still, the people ignored him, remaining hunched in the shadows, trying to stay invisible.

As Father Sama'an prayed for discernment for next steps to take, he sensed the Holy Spirit telling him to come back again, but to bring boots and a flashlight next time. He was not to give up. Time and again, he pointed his flashlight into the shadows and stepped into the stagnant air of the pens, looking for those hiding. "Come with me," he said, inviting them to help start a church in that forsaken place. He breathed in the smell of manure and rotting vegetable scraps. Still, they resisted, not looking him in the eye. "Take their hands and kiss them," Father Sama'an sensed from the Holy Spirit. "Kiss them on the head. Love them the way I love them."[15] Father Sama'an felt the Lord tell him to bring some shoes along next time—not for himself, but for those stuck in the mud and mire. With the servant's heart of Saint Sama'an, the one-eyed tanner, who had carefully fashioned shoes for the residents of that place in an earlier era, Father Sama'an was to give these people firm footing. There in the pens, he stooped low and slipped the shoes over their feet. Finally, they relented. Taking his hand, they walked out into the open space.

Father Sama'an and his co-laborers in the Lord continued to visit the huts one by one, preaching the gospel of repentance and grace to the people of Garbage City and inviting them to the church. With eleven people, they built a tin church with a roof of reeds to match the makeshift dwellings of the Zabbaleen. "It felt like the manger scene in Bethlehem," Father Sama'an said, laughing.[16] Five months later, the tin structure could no longer hold the congregation. So they enlarged the meeting place, adding walls of brick and concrete. On top of the walls, they positioned a canvas tarp, reminiscent of the tabernacle where God met with His people during Israel's sojourn through the desert.

In 1976, when they needed yet a more expansive place, the growing congregation began construction for a meeting place within the mountain, the very place where Father Sama'an had first prayed. Ten years later, they finished the world-famous cave church amphitheater, St. Sama'an Church, now the largest church in the Middle East. When Father Sama'an and friends built this permanent chapel in the rock once excavated to construct the pyramids of Giza, many observed that a feeling of stability and permanence spread from the church to the community of migrants. In the years since, the Zabbaleen have built permanent brick structures for their homes. Streets have been paved. And the people have built schools and clinics. The church has provided a foundation for these people. They are no longer wanderers.[17]

Over the years, the Zabbaleen have paired their work ethic with innovation and have increased income for themselves while providing an invaluable service to the city of Cairo. With a population of almost 18 million people, Cairo generates approximately 15,000 tons of waste each day. Trekking into Cairo before dawn every morning, the Zabbaleen team up to collect nearly 9,000 tons of that waste.[18] Using wooden carts pulled by donkeys, or sometimes old pickup trucks, the Zabbaleen collect more than two-thirds of all the trash in Cairo. Upon returning to their homes, they sort out the trash by hand. They recycle organic waste by feeding it to the pigs in their sties or turning it into compost. What they do with the plastic, metal, and other non-organic waste is just as impressive. Reporter Alan Kadduri says that in partnership with local manufacturers, "The output is eventually turned into quilts, rugs, pots, paper . . . recycled plastic products such as clothes hangers, and much more."[19] Trash to treasure is no cliché for these people.

The Zabbaleen are good at what they do—in more ways than one. Estimates affirm, "Reusing and recycling about 85% of all waste that they collect, the Zabbaleen have far surpassed the efficiencies of the best Western recycling schemes, which have so far only been able to reuse 70% of all material."[20] What others have discarded and deemed unusable, the Zabbaleen have harnessed and turned into a regular income for more than 50,000 living in Garbage City. Leader of the Zabbaleen union,

Ezzaet Naem, says, "Two are collecting from door to door. One is transporting. And two are sorting. . . . So it's 5 as a beginning. And another 7 indirect jobs are recycling paper, plastic, metal, glass. So each ton of garbage in Cairo is creating 12 jobs every day."[21] Plastic scraps can sell for $600 per ton, according to professional recycler Sherif El Ghamrawy. He says if done right, the revenue in the stigmatized trash and recycling industry can rival the salaries of some university graduates in Cairo.[22]

Naem says, "We have always been treated as a backward people incapable of managing the refuse of such a large town. And yet we are the ones who invented an eco-city model."[23] The Zabbaleen harness the resources around them and create their homes and buildings with a unique vision. Most set up recycling facilities on the ground floor with living quarters upstairs. Some contribute to an even more creative ecosystem by installing container gardens on the rooftop or powering the home with biogas generators fueled by garbage. Kadurri says that while the neighborhood is still messy, it has developed its own way of life in which the church is making an impact.[24]

Through teaming up with the church and nonprofits, citizens are getting an education. They practice reading, writing, and math. They're learning more effective recycling methods.[25] And they're learning how the Bible and a life of prayer can transform the way they look at their work. "No work is shameful. What's shameful is sitting at home and living off someone else, or begging for alms, or stealing," says garbage collector Gerges Saad. "But the Bible says if you work hard, you'll always have bread."[26] With these skills under their belts, and a new understanding of their value in the sight of the Lord, Zabbaleen believers are learning to step out from the margins, become their own advocates in society, and develop healthy, holistic ways to grow both their financial stability and their witness in the world.

As Christian businesspeople, these trash collectors can do their work as unto the Lord in a way that no other group in Cairo can. On their daily routes through the neighborhoods of Cairo, the Zabbaleen find inroads to share the way of Jesus. Once, when a lady accidentally threw her bag of jewelry away, a garbage collector, a follower of Christ, found it in the pile of trash. As quickly as possible, he returned it to its rightful owner. "Where does this honesty come from?" the woman asked. He replied, "Our Jesus taught us to be honest."[27]

These workers, though dirty and unkempt, demonstrate righteousness in their business. As John Warton says, when a Christian businessperson brings honor to Jesus through their work, that's a church growth strategy.[28] Driving all over the city of Cairo in their carts and trucks, the Zabbaleen interact on a daily basis with more of Cairo's 18 million people than any other ministry in the city. When a trash collector knows the Lord, he becomes a light to the whole city, Father Sama'an says, "God has chosen them to be a blessing for Egypt."[29]

True relief from the big problems of the world will come when those in underdeveloped places pair their own skills and resourcefulness with the unique opportunities for service in their home communities. Wherever we are, we can encourage ourselves and our fellow citizens to use our own local resources, even if those resources include garbage. And as Father Sama'an and the Zabbaleen have demonstrated, investing in the most vital resource of human ingenuity can transform trash into treasure.

GROUP-THINK

When you enter a place and seek to address its problems, is your first instinct to empower others or to make power plays? In 1 Corinthians 3:7–9, Paul writes, "So neither the one who plants nor the one who waters is anything, but only God, who makes things grow. The one who plants and the one who waters have one purpose, and they will each be rewarded according to their own labor. For we are God's coworkers in God's service" (NIV). If the God of the universe can allow us to be His coworkers, then surely we can team up with other humans to effect transformation. We do our part, other people do theirs, and God causes the increase.

You have a unique bundle of natural giftings, skills you've built through experience, and resources that are in your reach. Take a few minutes to jot down some of the gifts, skills, and resources God has provided for you. Set a time to meet with someone closely connected with the place or situation that has your attention. Ask that person if they'd be willing to make a similar list of their own gifts, skills, and resources. Then ask that person to make another list of what he or she envisions for the community. Put all three lists side by side, do some group-think, and see how you and others might team up to work toward that vision.

Like my friends who are working with refugees, investing in budding entrepreneurs, or empowering citizens to turn trash into treasure, we can say yes to teaming up for transformation. We can say yes to using the unique gifts God has given us, and we can say yes to engaging with the gifts He has given others. As we partner with other believers toward a common goal, and see God's kingdom come on earth, not only will we go deeper in our relationship with our Creator God, but we will go deeper in our connection with the many creative citizens He has placed in our communities. When we find our people and work together in tandem with the Lord, our efforts multiply and real change begins.

Stand Your Ground

Bowls and plates clattered against one another like the sound of chattering teeth. The ground quivered under our feet. Bombs thundered in the distance, lobbed by angry men demanding to be heard. All we heard were the explosions—and the gunshots. Every hard surface of our tiny home seemed to amplify the sounds of violence. Every brick, glass window slat, cement block, and ceramic tile gave a startled reaction to the fighting around us. Doris, our daughters, and I learned quickly how to dive for cover under our beds when we heard bullets flying by.

Just months earlier, we had flown down through the cottony clouds to the sight of the most lush tropical vegetation we'd ever seen. When we landed, our new local friends gave us a hearty welcome and led us on a grand tour of their beautiful city built on the sides of a volcano. Little did we know what was brewing beneath the surface of it all.

As we settled in, we began to hear strong words shouted over the loudspeaker of the local university. "Rise up!" the voices urged. "Stand against injustice!" Lack of access to land for all but an elite group, wide gaps between opportunities for the rich and poor, denials of basic freedoms, overreach by the military and government, villages attacked—all these things were like magma slowly boiling up to a full-on eruption of revolution.

Over the course of twelve years from 1979 to 1991, the civil war in El Salvador would kill 70,000 people in a nation of less than five million. Our survival was no guarantee. In the wake of the revolution, our family members in other Latin American nations begged us to leave our new home and church in order to seek safety. Eyes darting, our local friends would tell us how they'd leave for work in the morning unsure of whether they'd be coming home that evening. It was hard for us not to feel anxious, too.

Beginning with our days in Chicago, Doris and I had been learning to get comfortable with being uncomfortable. Through fasting, prayer, Bible study, and other spiritual disciplines, we were learning to lean into discomfort in order to find greater strength—deciding not to buy a house in Chicago when so many of our dear friends were putting down roots; trusting God to get me into seminary on short notice; giving up the steady life of the business world and instead balancing side jobs, ministry, and studies for extended periods of time; listening for His whispers about just what place and people we should adopt for our first pastoral assignment. Each scenario had come with its own type of anxiety.

Then one morning in San Salvador, a phone call jolted Doris out of her morning routine. Adalia, our faithful house helper, picked up the phone. As she put the receiver to her ear and said, "Digame," a gravelly voice interrupted.

"Luis has forty-eight hours to leave the country, or suffer the consequences," the voice threatened.

Adalia ran to tell Doris. Immediately, Doris went to our room and fell on her knees by the bedside, begging God for His mercy and wisdom. The situation was not to be taken lightly. We had known of whole families in San Salvador who had been forced to watch the execution of a loved one.

When I walked in the door that evening, I knew something was wrong. With passports and luggage ready, Doris told me of the death threat. It seemed we had no choice but to leave. Yet I couldn't imagine this was how God wanted our El Salvador assignment to end. Not this way, not now, when we were just getting started. From our time doing Bible study in the Chicago high-rise to the time that we glided down onto the lovely volcano that is San Salvador, as we said yes to God, we had been building a history with Him. It was like our own version of Psalm 136, each remembrance of His protection and provision followed by the refrain, "His steadfast love endures forever." But now, the stakes were getting higher. The next stanza of our life was in the crosshairs. We wanted to sing God's faithfulness in this place, but we didn't want to be foolish. It was a tough place to be—in more ways than one.

Though Doris and I had some practice in prayer and fasting up to that point, we still had to deal with our human reflexes, that famous fight-or-flight stress response. Should we stay or go? We didn't like the idea of living each day in fear, wondering when the mysterious caller might make good on his promise to hunt me down. But neither did we like the idea of being chased from a place we had been so sure we were called to.

FAITH OR FOOLISHNESS?

When the apostle Paul says, "We are fools for Christ's sake" (1 Cor. 4:10), he does not mean he and his fellow workers in the gospel are just plain fools. We should not assume every hardship is sanctioned by God, even if we do believe that for those who love Him, "all things work together for good" (Rom. 8:28). As we discern whether to run from difficulty or stay put, there is room for us to address our concerns. There is space for our questions. There is space for us to share our preferences with the Lord and each other.

Even Jesus Himself did His due diligence. He had already prophesied to His disciples details of His impending suffering and death. Yet He did not go lightly into the suffering before Him. In the garden of Gethsemane, as He was about to be betrayed, He cried out to God the Father for final assurance that He really should take up that cross and walk up the hill to certain death. Three times Jesus asked to be released from the weight of suffering:

Then he said to them, "My soul is very sorrowful, even to death; remain here, and watch with me." And going a little farther he fell on his face and prayed, saying, "My Father, if it be possible, let this cup pass from me; nevertheless, not as I will, but as you will." Again, for the second time, he went away and prayed, "My Father if this cannot pass unless I drink it, your will be done." So, leaving them again, he went away and prayed for the third time, saying the same words again. (Matt. 26:38–39; 42; 44)

He stood up from that sacred meeting knowing for sure that the cup of suffering would not pass from Him. And He walked willingly into what, from all other perspectives, looked like a death trap.

Doris and I knew we needed to inquire of God, to bring our preferences before Him, and to discern His will. With our suitcases still lined up by the door, I called the members of our church's elder board. That very night, they held a prayer meeting, wrestling for us until the morning light. When the sun peeked up over the horizon, they decided that we would move out of our home and into a hotel temporarily. When our time was up, Doris still didn't have peace about doing family life and ministry in such an explosive place. On our calendar, I pointed out an upcoming trip to neighboring Guatemala where I would be teaching a short course at a seminary. This would be the perfect opportunity for us to get away, devote some time in prayer as a couple, and to ask for God's clarity regarding our next steps.

As we searched Scripture together, Doris and I settled on several values that would inform our decisions from then on. We agreed that like Abraham and Sarah who lived as nomads, we would be willing to move whenever and live wherever God told us to go. We have moved eight times since. We agreed that in daily life we would be flexible, saying, "If the Lord wills, we will live and do this or that" (James 4:15). And we agreed to fully trust that our life, and even our death, is in the Lord's hands, saying, "Whether we live or die, we belong to the Lord" (Rom. 14:8 NIV). And we agreed that all other things pale in comparison to hearing our Savior say, "Well done, good and faithful servant" (Matt. 25:23). We returned to El Salvador with a new resolve to remain where God had assigned us, no matter the outcome. God gave us a framework for decision making to guide us through all of these years of worldwide ministry that would follow.

When we believers inquire of God, we receive either a new invitation to walk toward something different or an affirmation of the original invitation to walk forward with greater resolve. When we take up our cross, following Jesus, we can expect struggle to come our way. After all, that cross can look a lot like a target on our backs. The apostle Peter tells us, "Be alert and of sober mind. Your enemy the devil prowls around like a roaring lion looking for someone to devour" (1 Peter 5:8 NIV). Opposition doesn't always come as bullets whizzing by windows or death threats over the telephone. Sometimes opposition comes from the most unlikely places—from the inside, from those we thought were on our team. Such was the case for my friend Alex Philip.

THE GRAVEYARD

As we talked, Alex took his glasses down from his eyes and worked at the lenses with a soft cloth. Each time he retells the story of his early years of ministry, he sighs aloud. In 1992, he worked happily as a medical doctor in a hospital in Kerala, India. He had graduated with top honors in his studies and had just been invited to join the faculty of the institution where he was trained. Things were going as planned.

Then one day he received an unexpected call from back home.

When he picked up the handset, Alex received news that his father, a teacher and missionary, had passed into the presence of Jesus. Alex remembers fondly, and sometimes even laughs about, how his father's family devotions always inevitably ended with Matthew 28:18–20, the Great Commission. Whether the elder Mr. Philip would begin with a psalm or one of Paul's letters, he would always manage to bring the subject back around to: "Go therefore and make disciples of all nations" (v. 19).

This mission had so gripped Mr. Philip that he started a Bible school to train men and women for spreading the gospel throughout India. Now, Alex's father's earthly work was finished. As Alex made the two-day trip back south to visit his widowed mother and mourn his father's passing with the rest of the family, he began to rethink the trajectory of his life and career.

He remembers going into his father's office, opening the hefty drawers, and wondering what to do with all the files. He looked at all the correspondence, feeling both awestruck and sad, and sensed something. Just as he was about to return to the medical school, he received clear instructions to remain: "Don't go north. Stay here and pray for three months."[1]

Before learning of his father's death, Alex had been certain that he would join the faculty at the medical school. That's what he had worked toward. That's what he wanted. But God had said otherwise. And His was a voice that couldn't be ignored. Ultimately, whether pursuing medicine or ministry, Alex's desire was to do what God wanted him to do and go where God wanted him to go. So he agreed to stay and devote himself to prayer, unsure of what was to come.

One day during his three months of dedicated prayer, he received four different letters from four different people from four different parts of the world. All of them said, "Your father's mantle is upon you. Take it."[2]

It was then and there that he knew God was speaking back to him, answering his prayers. He put his medical degree away and began praying for next steps.

Alex and his wife, Laly, began studying statistics on the most impoverished part of India, the state of Bihar. They found that 39 percent of Bihari residents were living on less than a dollar a day. That research led Alex and Laly to leave the comfort of their home in Kerala, the southernmost state, with a 19 percent Christian population, and go north to Bihar where the population was 75 percent Hindu and 24 percent Muslim.[3]

"It was a clear directive for the Indian church to go to Bihar, the most backward, underserved area of the country," Alex said.[4] He and Laly took a sixty-hour train ride to what was known as "the graveyard of missions" and arrived to see the stats in real life. The children there were like the walking dead—naked, starving, dirty, and wracked with diseases.

Alex and Laly had come to plant churches in the forsaken cities and towns of Bihar, to bring hope and good news to a lost and suffering people. On their first night in Patna, the capital of Bihar, a dream came to both Alex and Laly individually as they slept, a dream that gave them a heart for a particular demographic in the area. In that dream, a choir of children held out their empty bowls and sang, "Give us bread."[5] And so God gave Alex and Laly a heart and a vision to nourish and nurture the children of Bihar. With that dream, God put a face to the problem that Alex and Laly could not ignore.

For the next three years, as Alex took the mantle of his father's ministry, he lovingly nurtured a group of cross-cultural missionaries, training them in poverty relief, helping them learn the local language, and teaching them the customs of the culture. He and Laly knew this is where God had called them. Alex used the ministry's entire budget to keep his staff on the field.

Then all but five of his ministry's staff left and took positions with other organizations right in town. "Maybe it was because I wasn't a very good leader," Alex said. "Maybe there were other organizations in the area that cherry-picked them, offering them $25 more or $50 more for their salaries."[6] Whatever the reason, this loss broke Alex's and Laly's hearts.

"These were our people. We had looked for the day when they would be able to speak the language, when they would be able to minister. And now almost all of them were gone," he said.[7] There was a heavy sense of betrayal in the months to follow. He didn't like feeling angry or disappointed. Alex wanted to get over it, but he didn't know how.

One evening, when his wife became ill, he looked out the window and sighed to himself, "Well, Bihar is called the graveyard of missions. Is it time for us also to leave?"[8] But then came an invitation to attend a small missions conference in the area. It was an invitation that came with a bit of hope that perhaps God would tell him something at the conference to strengthen him, to give him the resolve to move forward with his mission in Bihar. He needed something. So he went.

At the conference, he heard a testimony from George Otis about conflict between ministry leaders in another part of the world. He talked about a Bolivian man named Julio Ruibal and his wife who, around the same time that Doris and I moved to El Salvador, moved to pastor a church in Cali, Colombia, a place ruled by drug lords, gang violence, and organized crime rings. Sadly, when Julio began spending time with the other pastors in the area, he found them not much more likeable than the rest of the ruffian population. Julio became disillusioned with their attitudes and stopped attending the weekly gathering. But, as he entered into a time of intense fasting and prayer, he sensed from the Lord, "You don't have the right to be offended. You need to forgive."[9]

Alex listened as George Otis told how Julio went humbly to each pastor one by one to make things right, knowing that if the few Jesus followers in the area didn't work together in brotherly love, then they would likely never see transformation around them.

Somehow, this similar story, set in a different location and peopled with different characters, allowed Alex to see his own situation from a new perspective. Alex laughs about how he went to that meeting thinking God might say to him, "You mighty man of valor, God is with you," as the Lord had once said to Gideon. But instead God made it clear that he was to go back and forgive these people.[10] Rather than allow Alex to isolate himself in self-righteousness, God humbled him.

He went back home and called the four pastors from the other ministries in town, leaders he wouldn't dare talk to before, out of fear that they'd take more of his people. It had felt dangerous to be close to them. But with this assignment of reconciliation before him, he called them and invited them to breakfast at the local hotel.

"The conversation was as dry as the toast," Alex said. "There wasn't any trust. There wasn't any love. Nothing."[11] Alex wondered if he'd made a mistake. At the end of the meal, he wondered aloud, "Where do we go from here?" To his surprise, the pastors said they wanted to meet again the following month, and again after that. By the time they'd met for eight months, the group had grown to ten people. This was the place the pastors wanted to come now. As they warmed up to one another, they began to sit around the breakfast table and pray for one another. And, as Alex said, "When you pray for one another, you can't go and work against that pastor and feel a peace about it."[12]

When the pastors came together, Alex felt God at work in their unity. "As we sat with our fellow pastors and forgot about our differences, something happened," Alex said.[13] In this place where the per capita income was $35 USD per year, where starving children walked around barely clothed, where disease spread among the population, they began to notice little bits of progress. One would share a testimony of how God had provided a piece of land. Another would say God had blessed them with a new supporter. As the Lord blessed Alex's ministry from that point on, the staff grew from five to 150 in three years.

Alex began to see that there were deeper spiritual forces at work that wished to keep Bihar the graveyard of missions. In that desolate place that felt more like a mine field than a mission field, the enemy used dissension among believers to stall the work of God. But by listening and humbling himself, Alex let go of seeing other ministry leaders as the enemy. They weren't his competition. His real fight was "against the cosmic powers over this present darkness, against the spiritual forces of evil in the heavenly places" (Eph. 6:12), and he needed to stand his ground.[14]

PAIN AND GAIN

In Indonesia, where my friends Iman and Lea Santoso make their home, there is a prominent phrase in the culture. "Menerimanya," they say to one another. "Receive it." Pain is inevitable, but we turn our pain into misery when we resist it. When Indonesians use this phrase, they mean that we should live openhandedly, receiving whatever comes our way, without a spirit of panic or despair. Some psychologists may use the term "radical acceptance." Whatever its use in ancient or modern cultures, the concept of accepting adversity has long been a signpost on the path of faith. As Job asked when his wife begged him to renounce his faith in God and die, "Shall we accept good from God, and not trouble?" (Job 2:10 NIV) And the apostle Paul, survivor of multiple shipwrecks, beatings, and times of hunger, said,

> For I have learned to be content whatever the circumstances.
> I know what it is to be in need, and I know what it is to have
> plenty. I have learned the secret of being content in any and
> every situation, whether well fed or hungry, whether living in
> plenty or in want. I can do all this through him who gives me
> strength. (Phil. 4:11–13 NIV)

Just as Paul learned to be content in plenty or lack, we can go forward with an open posture, ready to receive whatever our mission brings upon us. Sometimes it may be suffering, sometimes joy, sometimes both at the same time.

Iman Santoso says that while he would never choose the violence and unrest his country experienced in the 1960s, it brought unprecedented spiritual openness. "There was chaos all around. Even my grandfather was on the hit list. Everywhere in Indonesia, people were fearful and restless," Iman said. "And they were seeking God. Relationships were close. People showed up at my door and came into my house twenty-four hours a day, seven days a week, to pray."[15] Because Christians turned to prayer instead of revenge, half a million former communists came to the churches looking for refuge, and many of them gave their lives to Christ.

Doris and I experienced something similar during our time in El Salvador. We saw a great spiritual openness as the excesses of life were peeled away and the people considered eternity—a natural response when death seems all too close. Believers sought God through much prayer and were ready to share their faith with frightened neighbors and friends. Living among these audaciously faithful people for seven years, Doris and I saw our own faith grow exponentially. We saw things we would never have witnessed if we had left. In fact, you probably wouldn't be holding this book if we hadn't stayed. The years that believers spent practicing and sharing the good news of Jesus in the middle of a war zone transformed the church. And that transformation contributed to the launch of the Latin American Mission Movement, which led to my engagement with Partners International and Lausanne, which led to the 10/40 Window Movement that swept the worldwide church into the modern missions era. God was at work, and we are thankful we were there to see it, as a result of saying yes to God's invitation to stand our ground.

As we committed to stay put in El Salvador, we had a clear

sense that while physical danger increased around us, the real battle was in the unseen world. One friend of ours, David Zavaleta, managed the Banco Agropecuario. Like me, he had received a death threat over the phone. Unsure of his eternity, this was a real wake-up call for him. Right away, he began to visit our church with his wife. I remember meeting him at his office once and watching him thumb through the letters on his desk from both the far-right and far-left political parties, each of which wanted him dead. As he prepared to leave for a business trip in New York during this time, a friend handed him a Bible. In his hotel room, far from the bombs and bullets where we were, he read it cover to cover. While David was off doing business in New York, he also did business with God, putting his life once and for all in Jesus' hands. When he came back, he had the look of peace on his face. He immediately began to comfort others with the comfort he had received, ministering to his distraught neighbors who were facing dangers in their everyday lives.

BEHIND THE HEADLINES

When the church is unified and in sync with God's Spirit, the culture at large begins to feel it, too—even in tumultuous times. In late January and early February 2011, many Egyptians in Cairo gathered at Tahrir Square (Freedom Square) to protest President Hosni Mubarak's thirty-year regime. They came with complaints about police brutality, emergency law, unemployment, and political corruption. Tanks flanked the thoroughfares of Freedom Square. Rioters and soldiers used tear gas, homemade bombs, knives, guns, bullets, rocks, and bottles—weapons of all kinds. Viciousness abounded.

But that's not the whole story. Author Sumbul Ali-Karamali shared her glimpse of beauty amid the chaos of the Tahrir protests. As she reported from her place in the middle of the action, she said, "I saw one of the most moving sights I have seen in a long time. The peaceful protests had turned violent, when armed pro-Mubarak mobs (likely instigated by the regime) began attacking unarmed protesters. But when the pro-Mubarak mobs started attacking Muslim Egyptians who were at their prayers in the square, Christian Egyptians made a ring around them to protect them as they prayed."[16]

Some of those Christians were members of Father Sama'an's congregation. Several days later, Muslims, in solidarity with Christians, returned the favor and formed a human ring around the Christians, protecting them as they participated in an outdoor Mass.

In November that same year, thousands of Egyptian Christians from various denominations gathered to pray in unity for Egypt. Many repented and renewed their relationship with the Lord. Seeing the Lord move among them, they felt bold to ask for more. In a vision, Father Sama'an had seen Jesus appearing over Tahrir Square. He sensed they and the Lord had something else to do there. He and his fellow church leaders asked God for another chance to pray in Tahrir Square, yet they did not know how to proceed.

As a minority group, Christians in Egypt have faced much persecution, ranging from losing valedictorian status at school to being gunned down during a church service. But the recent solidarity among Christians and Muslims brought hope.

"Should we ask permission from the army?" Father Sama'an and his fellow church leaders wondered aloud, "or the police?" With all the unrest, it was difficult to know who was in charge. Then one of the church leaders received a call from a female politician, with no religious affiliation, inviting the Christians to host a public gathering—at Tahrir Square. She promised to organize everything and acquire all the permissions. All they had to do was show up.

Gathering all these Christian leaders in one place, standing on a platform in the middle of Tahrir Square, was certainly dangerous. They were an easy target for a bomber or sniper in this tense political environment. Some of their relatives discouraged them from going. But the leaders felt they had a clear word from the Lord.

The night was December 31, 2011, the last day of this historic year for their nation. During the service, over a million people, predominantly Muslim, gathered in the square to protest all the corruption. The hour-long event was broadcast on major television channels, both secular and Christian. Priests and pastors led in prayer, praise, worship, Scripture readings, and short sermons. The main message given centered on the Christmas season and Emmanuel, God with us.

Many Muslims began to ask about the meaning behind Emmanuel and spoke of their longing for the God who is with us. In this Islamic country, out in public on a major square, under the media spotlights, our brothers and sisters in Egypt shared the good news of reconciliation, not only between those from different religious backgrounds, but also between humanity and God. The next morning, the newspaper reported the event. The headline read, "Christ in Tahrir Square." Father Sama'an's vision had become a reality.[17] The headlines would have read differently if our brothers and sisters in Cairo hadn't said yes to staying put amidst difficulty.

EVEN SO

If we are to combat injustice in the world and bring the light of Christ to dark places, we need to step close enough to feel the pain of the oppressed and afflicted. For the sake of others, we say yes to danger and hardship. And we can come out from the most harrowing of situations and still press on. We know that the "Lord laughs at the wicked, for he sees that his day is coming" (Ps. 37:13). We trust God will somehow work all things for good, but that does not mean we don't expect resistance. Wicked people will continue to say yes to evil. But we are committed to saying yes to Jesus, to exercising His authority in dark places.

Even as I write this, my friends and I are dealing with unexpected resistance in certain areas of the world. Some who oppose the gospel have made it difficult for nonprofits to continue feeding and educating children in local schools in one area of the 10/40 Window. But has the Lord led us here for nothing? We have been at this long enough to know resistance does not indicate we should leave the work so dear to our hearts—and to God's. While we don't have to seek out hardship, we, like Paul, can learn to be content whatever the circumstances, knowing that we will experience more of Christ's resurrection power (see Phil. 4:11).

Throughout my faith journey, I've noticed that a great

percentage of the Bible gives us narratives and instructions for how to navigate suffering. That tells me that a great percentage of our walk as believers will likely involve suffering, too. We must yearn and learn "to know Christ—yes, to know the power of his resurrection and participation in his sufferings" (Phil. 3:10 NIV). From the beginning when man brought brokenness into the world to the end when God redeems all creation, we see God protecting and sustaining His people and His world despite the havoc we, who sinned against Him, and the enemy have caused.

Our perspective determines how we interpret the trials we face, and what we see around us. If we focus on our pain, we will see darkness and gloom. In The Message, Hebrews 12:18 says, "Unlike your ancestors, you didn't come to Mount Sinai— all that volcanic blaze and earthshaking rumble—to hear God speak." Hebrews 12:22 goes on, "No, that's not your experience at all. You've come to Mount Zion, the city where the living God resides." And He is the One whose presence helps us to "count it all joy . . . when [we] meet trials of various kinds" (James 1:2).

What resistance are you experiencing in your efforts to help others right now? What emotions are rising to the surface as you face difficulty? Do you fear harm that may come your way as you enter into an unstable environment? Are you frustrated by conflict within a group that you once trusted? Have you felt betrayed or abandoned by a friend or co-laborer in the gospel? Have you second-guessed something that you felt God had invited you to do? How different might the situation look if you imagine yourself the sole representative of Jesus in that place?

The resistance you experience could be an indicator that God is doing something special and that His enemy wants to stand in the way. Commit yourself to standing your ground, and you'll see God's glorious story unfold, which is but a hint of the final glory to come. If we focus on the joy set before us, our faith and work will be more informed by the good ahead than the gloom here and now. And in spite of all the chaos that may come along the way, we can say with the apostle John, "Amen. Come, Lord Jesus" (Rev. 22:20).

Celebrate Your Chain Reaction

Paparazzi clicked and flashed their cameras as attendees pulled up in their cars to pack the opera house. Notable actors, artists, business moguls, and public officials walked the red carpet in flowing gowns and tailored suits. The scene looked something like Hollywood's Walk of Fame. But this wasn't the Oscars. There would be no award given for Best Picture here. The emcees at this awards ceremony in Kiev readied the stage to present something even better.

In that grand hall, the people of Ukraine gathered to recognize a most inspiring story—not on screen, but in real life. When the emcees revealed the winner of the 2012 Pride of the Country award at the end of the evening, they called out the most unlikely of names: the Isaev family.

A few years earlier, this name either would have been ignored or raised the eyebrows of those who heard it. But now, as Evgeniy Isaev, his wife, Svetlana, and their kids took to the stage, the attendees erupted in applause and tears. Their children, who had once been considered the lowest of society, now watched the crowd give them a standing ovation.

Evgeniy Isaev at first clapped his hands together, but very quickly moved them to cover his face, holding back tears in the gravity of the moment. With his wife at his side and their children arranged like stair steps in front of them, he thought about the journey they had taken to adopt so many little ones, how these HIV-positive orphans had become sons and daughters. He thought about the milestones along the way as he and Svetlana set out to grow this unconventional family in a place where even the healthiest orphans were viewed with suspicion.

What not many people know is that less than a decade earlier, Evgeniy and Svetlana were considered failures. In his late teens, Evgeniy had lived the party life, trying every kind of drug that came across his path. At nineteen, Evgeniy came down with what seemed to be a respiratory sickness and when he had to be taken to the emergency room, tests came back showing that he didn't have just any virus—he had HIV. Those three letters sounded like a death sentence to him.[1]

Elsewhere, Svetlana was wrapped up in problems of her own. Steve Weber, who serves with Christian Broadcasting Network and World Without Orphans in Ukraine, remembers his close friend Genady telling how Evgeniy and Svetlana separately found their way to the steps of a rehabilitation center in their region. "One of them was in handcuffs and the other one had a hole in his head, was strung out on drugs, and was HIV positive. Now they are the pride of Ukraine."[2] What happened between those two drastic scenes?

"I began to search for God," Evgeniy said.[3] One verse in particular took residence in his mind: "But seek first the kingdom of God and his righteousness, and all these things will be added to you" (Matt. 6:33). Evgeniy gave himself fully to God and soon met his future wife, Svetlana. Growing up, the thought of marrying an HIV-positive man would've seemed like a nightmare to Svetlana. Yet, in her newfound faith, she began dreaming of creating a life with Evgeniy.

Still, there were risks and repercussions. After they were married, Svetlana's boss fired her, citing her close relationship with an HIV-positive person. But Svetlana felt confident that no matter what discrimination or difficulty she would face, there was a special plan for her and Evgeniy. Once married, through the safest methods possible, Evgeniy and Svetlana conceived twins. Tragically, one of the twins was stillborn. During her extended stay in the hospital, Svetlana waited for healing, both physical and emotional. It was during that time of quietness that God gave her a new dream.

Evgeniy tells the story: "Sveta came to me and said, 'Let's adopt a little boy, only not a normal little boy.' I said, 'What do you mean by not normal—from the moon or what?' She said, 'No, [a little boy] with the same diagnosis as you.'"[4] Evgeniy needed no convincing.

In 2007, the Isaevs became the first family in the history of Ukraine to adopt an HIV-positive orphan. This stigmatized couple invited another stigmatized individual into their family. I suppose they figured that if you're going to be stigmatized, you might as well really go for it. And go for it they did. Today, the Isaevs have eleven children—two biological and healthy, two adopted and healthy, and seven adopted and HIV-positive.

Svetlana says, "If you are walking with God and say yes to

Him, He will give you the desires of your heart."[5] Not only that, if you say yes to God, even when others disapprove of your decision, He just might change your heart's desire, change the dynamic of your family, and even use you to change a nation, like He did with the Isaevs.

At the awards ceremony, Anna Herman, Advisor to the President of Ukraine, leaned down to give each Isaev child a hug and kiss, an act of affection that once would have drawn gasps from horrified citizens who feared orphans, especially those with HIV.[6] Through this family saying yes to living through stigma, and through a small group of concerned friends who gathered in a living room to pray for a Ukraine without orphans, the orphan movement in Ukraine has now been brought to center stage—literally.

In the few years since the Isaevs received national recognition, and in a time of great uncertainty and unrest in Ukraine, the nation has experienced remarkable unity as leaders have prioritized the cause of the orphan. This movement has seen a turnaround not only in the public image of the orphan, but also in the relationships between various traditions and denominations of the church. Two in particular put aside a long-term feud to unite and champion the cause of orphans. In 2012, the Moscow Patriarchate sent out letters to every church in approximately 13,000 parishes, urging their flocks to pray for orphans on Orphan Sunday. Along with many catalysts from Ukraine Without Orphans, the Moscow Patriarchate later invited Steve Weber (Orphan Challenge Facilitator for Transform World) and Ruslan Maliuta (former candidate from Ukraine to the UN Committee on Rights of the Child) to host the day of

prayer for orphans inside Perchersky Lavra, the Moscow Patriarchate's main monastery. Outside, the congregation gathered
to release thousands of balloons as a symbol of their prayers to
God for the orphans in their nation.

In November 2014, the Moscow Patriarchate gathered with
the *other* Ukrainian Orthodox church, the Filaret, Kyivskaya
Patriarchate. The two are historically anathema to one another,
yet for this cause they stood together on the same platform.
Leaders from other traditions and denominations stood with
them as well. Even in the unrest after the annexation of Crimea,
Christian leaders, secular leaders, and a great crowd of citizens
gathered in St. Michael's Square to make the cause of the orphan a national priority. Together they asked God to forgive
them for anything they've done that has increased the number
of orphans in their nation. Our friend Roman Korneyko of
Ukraine Without Orphans prayed into the microphone and
out over the crowd with great fervor, "We repent, heavenly
Father, for our sins and for the iniquities of our forefathers, for
our part in destroying families, for adultery, and for abortion."[7]
Father Guzar, leader of the Roman Catholics in Ukraine, expressed for the assembly that the name Ukraine Without Orphans is a statement of faith for the nation.

Even Ukraine's First Lady, Maryna Poroshenko, took to the
platform and shared her heart about the matter at hand: "My
dream is that in Ukraine, there will be no more abandonment
and that in our hearts, the love of neighbors and our relatives
would prevail. I ask all Ukrainians to remember each day that
there are always children beside us who are in need of our
attention and care." She went on to pray, "God give us strength

and zeal to pray and do everything necessary to ensure that children are not abandoned and that, by Your help, orphans would receive the families they desire in their hearts."[8] And then she released a white dove into the air as a symbol of their unified prayer.

Sometimes we have goals for widespread transformation and plans for how to get there, but we may find God working in a counterintuitive way. We may think that in order to inch toward our dream of a nation without orphans, we need to start at the top and convince those in power to do something. But sometimes God starts in the dregs of society. Sometimes He starts in the dirt where the roots take hold. Should it surprise us, though? Hasn't God told us He likes to work this way? As the apostle Paul tells us, "God chose the foolish things of the world to shame the wise; God chose the weak things of the world to shame the strong" (1 Cor. 1:27 NIV). God has used a small band of advocates in Ukraine to prompt not only a national movement, but a worldwide anthem.

Remember how women in Ukraine once put pillows in their bellies to feign pregnancy to avoid the ridicule and shame that came along with adopting an orphan? Now, families who adopt are treated with respect and care. As a result of these few pioneering believers, congregations in Ukraine now rally around families who choose to adopt, helping them meet their increased food, clothing, and medical needs, and providing them emotional and spiritual support when they face challenges. These days, adoption is becoming an honor. Having witnessed such profound transformation in their society, our friends at Ukraine Without Orphans press on toward the day when believers in Jesus will empty the orphan system in their nation. The story of the Isaevs' journey from the curb to the stage and the story of Ukraine's once-calloused heart now beating strong for the orphan shows me that even the most hopeless situations can be transformed when a small group of faithful believers say yes to God—even when it appears to be scandalous.

SHOUT OUT

Remember signing yearbooks at the end of the school year and picking who was most likely to win the Nobel Peace Prize, become a rock star, or travel the world? If you had to guess the most likely future for a little boy born to a Buddhist family near Seoul, South Korea, who worked for his parents' local store and rice farm, what "most likely" category would you pick?

When the Korean War began in 1950, that little boy and his family were forced to leave their life and livelihood behind. They walked more than five hundred miles to safety, eating grass and even tree bark to keep from starving. Later, as a young man, Nam Soo Kim survived serving in the military and then dealt with multiple failures in the business world. At his coming of age, he couldn't seem to find the peace Buddhism promised. Twisted with anxiety and laid low with despair, he found himself on the brink of suicide.

With nowhere else to turn, he wandered into the evening service at a local church. That night, as if by sudden revelation, he became utterly convinced of God's existence. Like Isaiah in the presence of God, Nam Soo Kim found himself feeling like an undone man (see Isa. 6:5). Though the earth had always been full of the holiness and glory of the Lord, Nam Soo Kim was just now sensing it. And in the presence of God, Nam Soo Kim became convinced of the fact that God had a purpose for keeping him alive.

For the next six months, if the church doors were open, Nam Soo Kim was there, usually weeping in his seat. "My handkerchief was always wet," he said of the early days of faith.[9] Day and night he cried, crushed and repentant before God. His family jeered at this new direction in his life. *Had he lost his mind?* they thought. Then the unthinkable happened, sending the family into a panic. Nam Soo Kim's younger brother received a shocking diagnosis. The doctors said it was leukemia with no hope for a cure.

Nam Soo Kim knew the change his Savior had made in him during recent months, and he knew the power Jesus had demonstrated during His ministry on earth. "I am the resurrection and the life," Jesus had told the panicked sisters of dead Lazarus. "Whoever believes in me, though he die, yet shall he live" (John 11:25). Jesus had raised the widow's son, the daughter of Jairus, Lazarus, and even Himself from the dead. Nam Soo Kim knew Jesus had power over sin, sickness, and death. He knew Jesus' power could quicken the heart and lungs and cells and organ systems of his brother's body. So he did all he knew to do. He prayed.

He prayed that God would write a testimony in the medical record of his dying brother, and that that testimony would do more than just bring his brother back from the brink of death. He prayed that it would transform his whole family. Boldly, Nam Soo Kim challenged his family to accept Jesus as Savior if his brother received a complete healing. In their desperation, they accepted the challenge. What did they have to lose?

He took his dying brother up to Prayer Mountain near the demilitarized zone, a buffer land between North and South Korea established at the end of the Korean War. This place carries on the tradition of the persecuted Koreans of the late 1800s who fled to the mountains to cry out to God, a place that provided solace during war, a place where Christians from all over the world now go to seek God.[10] Nam Soo Kim knew it was the perfect place for audacious prayer.

Whether praying alone or in a group, Korean Christians pray out loud—with an emphasis on loud. They literally shout, blasting like trumpets, crying out to God in harmony with one another and with no sense of bashfulness, awkwardness, or propriety. Nam Soo Kim was no different. He and his family were desperate, and Nam Soo Kim knew where to direct that desperation.

For seven days, he prayed over his brother, begging God to perform a miracle. He wanted God to work. Soon, he started thinking God might. Then he started knowing God would. And three months later, the doctors flipped to the last page of his brother's medical file and scribbled an unexplainable word: "CURED."[11]

Nam Soo Kim's personal faith had started a chain reaction of faith that couldn't be stopped. One changed man believed and confessed Jesus as Savior. That same man accepted God's invitation to pray audaciously. That man's brother moved from certain death to abundant life. Wide-eyed and full of gratitude, Nam Soo Kim's family left behind Buddhism and embraced Jesus. And that was just the beginning.

Encouraged by the miraculous transformation in his family, Nam Soo Kim made a simple promise to God: "I will follow You."[12] In the years ahead, both brothers would follow the call to share Jesus in distant places, the uttermost parts of the earth, multiplying the reach of the gospel. After graduating from Bible school, Nam Soo Kim and his wife started a church in the slums of Seoul. Finding themselves in the same financial position as those in the community, they fasted much of the time due to limited resources. In his hunger, Nam Soo Kim recalled the difficulty of childhood days, surviving on grass and tree bark. But now he had his faith in the Lord and his vision for kingdom work sustaining him.

From there, he, his wife, and their girls made their way to a remote village in Vietnam in the early 1970s. Knowing what God had done with Nam Soo Kim's brother, they would follow Him anywhere, even to treacherous places. They felt strongly that they needed to say yes to this invitation, knowing that to get to the place where God wants you to ultimately be, you must first follow where He leads in the moment.

"There was constant tension in Vietnam," Nam Soo Kim's fellow missionary, John Hurston, wrote, "and all the missionaries who served on our team knew the conditions before they joined us. They were a devoted breed, committed to Paul's principle that the enemy cannot kill us until God is through with us."[13] So follow they did, right into the war zone.

But by 1975, as American troops pulled out of the Vietnam War and the North Vietnamese took over, Nam Soo Kim's family found themselves stuck with no money or transportation to flee the aftermath. And they had no way to contact anyone to let them know of their situation. All they could do was send desperate prayers to One who doesn't require wires or signals to receive calls. They knew He would hear them. They knew He would help.

The next morning, an American doctor from a local hospital showed up and told the family to pack their bags. As it turns out, the American government had arranged a special flight to airlift the doctor out of Vietnam, but he had suddenly thought of Nam Soo Kim's family. Nam Soo Kim saw this not just as a rescue, but an invitation. And he knew to say yes.

This was just one more event in the chain reaction that God would use to expand his discipleship and evangelistic influence. After an interim stay in Europe, he and his family accepted an invitation to go to Manhattan. As he made the journey, Nam Soo Kim sensed God was telling him to plant a church. Nam Soo Kim thought back to the simple promise his family made to follow God and allow Him to transform their lives if He granted them a miracle. And so Nam Soo Kim named this new congregation Promise Church.

As soon as he began the work of pastoring his fellow Koreans in the area, God's Spirit began to move, and the church began to grow. At first, there was one service, then there were two services, then three, then four. Faster than they could add more chairs, the church filled with people who, like Nam Soo Kim in his early months of faith, were weeping in repentance when faced with God's holiness. Testing the limits of the building's capacity, this dedicated and growing group of Korean believers had to move to a bigger facility.

But they were not meant to stay within those walls. There

was ministry to do beyond their doorstep. This Korean-American congregation began to meet families from all languages and cultures in the surrounding area. They tuned in to the personality of the neighborhood and found a meeting point between the gifts and passions of the members of the congregation and the needs of local families. Soon the church opened its doors on Saturdays to provide Power House, a free enrichment program for neighborhood children. Drummers, guitarists, violinists, and pianists offered classes to train kids in their particular musical instrument. Athletes coached table tennis, soccer, basketball, and many other sports. Artists taught drawing, painting, and ceramics. As soon as Promise announced the program, over a thousand people registered. Every Saturday to this day, parents and children flock to Promise Church for an hour of singing, dancing, and Bible study, followed by an hour of enrichment classes.

Promise Church can be described as an innovative, creative, go-getter church with seemingly boundless energy and generosity. They have discovered a dependence on God that allows them to think beyond the challenges in front of them, to do big, brave things with quiet, humble attitudes.

Building on their concept of blessing local families and children with enriching experiences, Promise Church felt led to extend this same idea to children in underdeveloped countries. In recent years, they have brought songs and dancing, and coordinated to bring world-famous soccer teams to stadiums in nations where children have never seen a live game played by professionals.

On one trip to Venezuela, a country where everything from

freedom of business to freedom of religious expression has been squelched, Nam Soo Kim marveled that the local government officials gladly provided personal transportation for the Promise team to and from the stadium. Nam Soo Kim's people went in with a servant's heart and an attitude of humility, and God granted them favor with the local authorities. Nam Soo Kim and his people offer something of great value, not only to believers, but also to communities as a whole. Even if a government opposes and outlaws faith, believing God to be a myth or a threat, you'd be hard-pressed to find anyone that could resist the gifts that His Spirit brings.

As Nam Soo Kim and his team come in and put on a top-notch event, they humbly and boldly demonstrate Jesus' love for thousands of children in underprivileged areas. In one particular case, the respectful relationship with the otherwise oppressive government allowed the message of hope to extend beyond the stands of the stadium in Venezuela.

Under Chavez's political strategies and executive orders, which transformed Venezuela into a communist nation, churches were forced to quiet their expression of faith. But the bold joy of a few can be contagious, leading to the boldness of many. As many adult Christians cowered in their homes, afraid to exercise their faith publicly, something was happening in the stadium full of exuberant children. There, 700,000 children stomped their feet on the bleachers and raised their hands in the air as they sang songs of Jesus' love. Cameras perched on scaffolding documented the joy on their faces, broadcasting the rally on television. And not just any television—we're talking about government-owned television. Yes, this station broadcast a rally about Jesus to 150 million viewers in a nation that had been squelching free exercise of religion.

Nam Soo Kim heard reports that believers at home on their couches rose up to their feet in shock. "Something has changed," they gasped. "Something is happening!"[14] These children, seemingly unfazed by the oppression around them, responded in pure joy to the happy atmosphere in the stadium. Venezuela is still hurting. Shelves and bank accounts are empty. But there is hope that these precious children may ten years down the road open the door for the gospel to bring peace, contagious joy, and overflowing abundance to their nation.

When I think back on Nam Soo Kim weeping in his seat at church as a young man, and then contrast it with this recent scene from the stadium in Venezuela, Psalm 126:5–6 comes to mind: "Those who sow in tears shall reap with shouts of joy! He who goes out weeping, bearing the seed for sowing, shall come home with shouts of joy, bringing his sheaves with him." And that same harvest gives seed that will itself be planted, springing up in new growth as the seasons move along. Because of his individual yes and the yes of his family, because of saying yes to hunger and dangerous mission assignments, and because of the yes of his congregation in blessing children and families all over the world, we may never see an end to this particular chain reaction.

WAKE UP THE DAWN

But what about those who came before and planted churches, making a way for that suicidal young man to know the Prince of Peace? Nam Soo Kim's chain-reaction story starts before his time. He and my other South Korean friends come from a robust Christian community in their home country, one that has developed through great hardship and overflowed into the missions force worldwide. The hearty faith of South Korea goes hand in hand with the thriving economy and public sphere. South Korea ranks in the top three economies of Asia, in the top ten economies worldwide, and is one of the most technologically advanced nations. Unlike the policies of their neighbors in North Korea, South Korea benefits from scriptural values that have influenced the way the nation conducts everyday life, bringing freedom and flourishing. South Korea is such a shining city on a hill, that its development is commonly known as "Miracle on the Han River."[15] But not so long ago, in the days during and after the Korean War, South Korea itself was one of the poorest nations in Asia.

Through another South Korean friend of mine, Young Gil Lee, I have been introduced to a man named Yong Ki Kim, who blazed the trail for South Korea to flourish. As he looked at the wasteland around him, he may have for a split second thought that South Korea was a hopeless cause. But that's certainly not where his mind stayed. He believed that the God who hovered over the darkness of the waters in Genesis could bring new life to the toxic dust of his land. "When you transform the land, you transform the nation," Kim heard in his heart. Just as Joshua and Caleb saw milk and honey instead of giants, Yong Ki Kim saw that God had good things in store for his nation, despite the dire future that some would paint. This forsaken place could one day produce life. But it would take pioneers with a problem-solving mentality to believe the vision and march onward.

Starting in 1931, Yong Ki Kim began tilling the ground, both physically and spiritually, preparing the soil for what would someday come to be known as the Canaan Farmers Movement. When Yong Ki Kim toured Korea and considered the barren landscape and weary people before him, every place around him seemed desolate. The original site of the Canaan Farmers Movement, Whang San Ri, carried the curse in its name, literally translated as "a desolate mountain village." The earth was acidic. Vegetable seeds planted in that soil would wither and fail to grow to fruition. Same for the fruit trees planted on the mountainside. But as families began to steward the land together, using appropriate methodologies to amend the soil, slowly the desolate mountain began to hold and nurture life again. Now the village has changed its name to Poong San Ri, "a rich mountain village."

Over the years, Kim developed five agricultural communities, teaching people how to work the land and to do so with joy. For this to happen, he said the people needed to shift from laziness to industriousness, from dependence to diligence, and from lack of cooperation to cheerful collaboration.

"Let's wake up the dawn," he told his co-laborers.[16] He'd get up at four o'clock in the morning, ring the bell to wake up the rest of the workers, begin the day in prayer and singing, then take to the field with a hoe in hand. This was not a movement for the fainthearted, or at least not for those who wished to stay that way. Leaders from surrounding villages began to notice the willing workers and abundant crops of Kim's community, and asked that Kim and his people share the secret to their motivation, exuberance, and success. He cheered his friends and followers on, saying things like, "Pioneers must sweat and weep" and, "Take courage, my country."[17]

As the Canaan Farmers model began to catch on, in the early 1960s, the president of South Korea, Park Chung-Hee visited the village to see what the rumors were all about. It is reported that he told Elder Kim, "My goal is to help our people and our country live well. But Mr. Kim, you have realized it already!"[18] In the days to follow, inspired by Kim's example, President Park would begin South Korea's New Village Movement.

Seeing the fruit of the Canaan Farmers Movement, the president trusted that with a little investment, the work ethic and ingenuity of his people would lead to abundance. So he provided every village across the nation with hundreds of bags of cement, half a ton of rebar, and some ideas. Each community followed the preliminary plan to select leaders, gather money, and coordinate village planning meetings. Then, the villagers got to work on fixing up homes, creating cultural centers, and working together to start business ventures that would serve their unique communities. Soon after, neighboring villages began partnering with each other to further spread the transformation that had started with the heart and work ethic of one man named Yong Ki Kim.[19] Dennis Sawyers of the Borgen Project reports that within a decade of the initiative, "rural income nearly sextupled from a household average of 225,800 won to 1,531,800 won. Thatched huts gave way to tiled houses across the country. Rural poverty decreased from 27.9 percent before the program to 10.8 percent after, and women gained a more prominent place in the local economy."[20]

Since the 1990s, the Canaan Farmers Movement has moved

beyond the borders of South Korea to other wastelands of the world, in nations such as Bangladesh, China, India, Indonesia, Myanmar, Palestine, the Philippines, and Uganda. The Canaan Farmers School location in South Korea has now trained over 700,000 people from Korea and 600 individuals from other nations in how to implement this transformative way of life in their own regions. It has produced such fruit, literally and figuratively, that the United Nations has recognized it as a highly respected example of transformative communities and has partnered with the school to train more farmers worldwide.[21]

This man and his small group of would-be farmers didn't set out to change the world, only to change their corner of it. But their work, done in tandem with their Creator, turned into expansive influence as those around them saw the transformation.

REASON TO CHEER

Stories of transformation aren't reserved for regions inside the 10/40 Window. We all have a chance to be part of a chain reaction. It starts with saying yes to the open invitation from God to lean into Him and find His heartbeat. When a small group of Jesus followers faithfully engages the problems in front of them, it starts a chain reaction from one place in history that will come to fruition at a future point in time. Coming generations reap the fruit of those who first said yes to tending the earth and filling it with God's glory. We witness a sequence of transformation that ultimately leads to praise and celebration.

When Jesus began His earthly ministry, He walked into the synagogue where He had grown up in Nazareth, unrolled a scroll and began reading the words of the prophet Isaiah,

"The Spirit of the Lord God is upon me, because the Lord has anointed me to bring good news to the poor; he has sent me to bind up the brokenhearted, to proclaim liberty to the captives, and the opening of the prison to those who are bound; to proclaim the year of the Lord's favor" (Isa. 61:1).

This prophecy, He told the congregation, had just been fulfilled in their presence (Luke 4:21). He was the One sent to actualize these promises. The passage in Isaiah goes on to reveal how God brings both emotional restoration ("the oil of gladness instead of mourning, the garment of praise instead of a faint spirit," v. 3), and physical restoration of community structures ("They shall build up the ancient ruins; they shall raise up the former devastations; they shall repair the ruined cities, the devastations of many generations," v. 4). Those who embrace Christ have inherited this blessing and this ministry of building up, raising up, and fixing up. We can be confident that when we practice faithful engagement with God in the places where He has stationed us, we will see transformation.

In the 10/40 Window, we've seen so much fruit from our labor. We've seen villages move from starvation to abundant harvest. We've seen a nation's orphans move from abandonment to honor. We've seen tension between ethnic groups melt away in prayers of repentance and reconciliation. Though we know we won't see full restoration until the Lord returns and redeems all creation, we have much to celebrate here and now.

Thinking back on all that I've witnessed makes me feel like one of the kids stomping in the bleachers at Nam Soo Kim's stadium events. As we celebrate what God has done in our lives and in the lives of those around us, let's retrace our steps to remember what things were like before and what resistance and challenges, sacrifice and suffering we met along the way. All of us have endured, and will continue to endure, great difficulty. But may we always rejoice in the Lord. "For as the earth brings forth its sprouts, and as a garden causes what is sown in it to sprout up, so the Lord GOD will cause righteousness and praise to sprout up before all the nations" (Isa. 61:11).

You don't need to be part of an established ministry to harness the energy of a chain-reaction story. In fact, our Transform World movement has chosen not to become an official organization precisely because we believe, as our friend Tim Keller said, that movements are "more grass roots, dynamic, and collaborative. Movements are dynamic, self-propagating, and encouraging to others to start similar efforts, without owning them" while organizations are "more top-down, structured, and controlling."[22] There is no membership when it comes to our movement. We are simply a group of committed people who trust and respect one another and apply our gifts and creativity to God's common calling in our lives. So, whether formal or informal, I encourage you to gather with like-minded friends in your circle and spur one another in putting steps to your faith and passions. Reporting to others about your steps in God's mission for you will give you a sense of accountability and keep you pressing forward to see more of the Lord's work in your area of impact.

Chain reactions always seem to bring on more chain reactions. When we celebrate one, often another unfolds. What chain reactions have you seen where one small yes after another has changed the course of history for an individual, family, neighborhood, or city? How might you celebrate that story and encourage the development of another? There are plenty of creative ways you might use to share the details of your personal yes effect. Perhaps you could write a blog post based on your own story of transformation or one in your community. Perhaps you could interview an adventurous believer you know and edit a video to share online. Or you could gather statistics and photographs to create an infographic featuring the before and after details of a particular situation in your area. You might display materials in a gallery and host an event to share what you've seen God do. Perhaps you could arrange a dramatic production communicating the transforming work your community has seen. Or you could host a music night weaving together songs, prayer, and an old-fashioned open mic testimony time. The opportunities are endless.

But maybe you're still waiting to experience your own chain-reaction story. In reading these stories, what element of the chain-reaction sequence do you find lacking in your own narrative? Like the people you've met in these pages, have you ever been truly overwhelmed by the holiness of God? Have you experienced the deep sorrow over your sin that comes to light in God's presence? Have you buckled over in desperate prayer? Have you listened for the Lord's direction? Have you followed through? Have you worked with an attitude of cooperation with the believers in your church or with the citizens of the surrounding community? Have you committed to seeing the task through to the finish, even through hardship? Have you felt the momentum that comes from knowing for sure God's Word will accomplish what He sends it out to do? What is missing for you?

God opens us up to His transformation plan by first offering to transform us. Little by little, He presents us with new opportunities to grow. He offers to sensitize our hearts, to give us His vision, to push us out and move our feet forward, to show us how to do our part and leave room for others to do the same, and to strengthen us through long-suffering. Then, He gives us an invitation to look back on what He has accomplished in and around us, giving us a glimpse of what's to come. And finally, He sends us back to our meaningful work with renewed vigor. As Isaiah 55:12 says, "For you shall go out in joy and be led forth in peace."

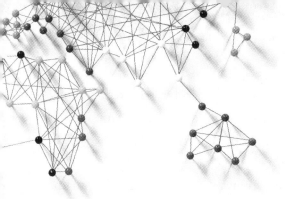

Lead Your Followers

I seemed to experience all of my childhood milestones a little late. My three brothers were standing tall in their first birthday photos, but mine shows me sitting down. It took me a while to get the hang of walking, along with a whole list of other things. I wasn't much for reading, writing, and arithmetic. I didn't have the gift of sitting still at my desk or the dinner table. And I didn't have the physique to make my mark in the athletic arena. As a youngster, when I tried to join in on playing soccer, the kids looked at me and made up a new chant to shout in unison. "Half-a-kilo, half-a-kilo," they jeered, which basically meant "scrawny."

I wasn't a natural at much of anything, but my advantage was that I had somebody watching out for me. My mother, who had heard the jeers on the field, started feeding me two lunches a day to bulk me up. In the margin next to my lackluster grades, teachers at school would write, "He tries hard, but just doesn't have it together." My mother would look at me and say, "Lou, you will be what you want to become." She'd keep saying it when I'd come back from making mischief with my neighborhood friends. Even when the officer showed up at my door and listed off all of my pranks and offenses, my mother offered forgiveness and spoke hope for my future. She was always a life-giver.

There were many temptations to let my God-given strengths morph into weaknesses, but the strong and gracious nurture I received in childhood kept me rooted and ready for the Word of the Lord. At night, my mother would tuck me in bed, kneel next to me, and fold her hands as I folded mine. Together, we would pray for our family members. Then, we would pray a familiar refrain, "Gentle Jesus, meek and mild, give a little child a place in the kingdom of your grace." Like me, every healthy, happy contributor to the good of society has someone who loved them fiercely and helped them stand, walk, and find their potential through growing pains—whether in childhood or later in life.

In the midst of extreme poverty, my Ethiopian friend Shiferaw Michael recalls how the lavish love of his mother gave him a secure foundation for dealing with the growling stomach and threadbare clothing of his childhood. Though his mother had her hands full trying to keep her eight children fed and clothed, Shiferaw remembers how she would take his face into her hands, look him in the eye, and speak love and life into him. Other parents in the culture would choose a harsh approach to the difficulties of family life and—in moments of frustration or despair—curse the day their children were born. But Shiferaw's mother wouldn't dare let her children think they were a burden—not for a minute. "Some cows have very long horns," his mother would tell him. "But however big they may be, they'll never be a burden for the cow. They are part of her."[1] Taking care of her children was a natural outflow of her love, and though Shiferaw would someday realize that he and his family were well below the poverty line, he grew up feeling no lack.

UNTAPPED RESOURCES

Now, with a father's heart, when Shiferaw Michael speaks of the poverty, malnutrition, poor sanitation, and disease of his home country and continent, you can see the veins pulsing in his clasped hands. He wants to look right into the face of his people and say, "You are not a burden. You are not a drain. You have the most lavish resources in reach. Use them." Shiferaw shakes his head and tells me, "It seems ridiculous to me that Africa is poor. It should be impossible to be poor in Africa, as far as resources are concerned. Africa is probably the richest continent when it comes to natural resources. Gold, diamonds, petroleum, salt, cocoa beans—we've got everything. So it is inexplicable to me as to why we remain the most miserable people on earth with everything we need to lead a better life right under our feet. Africa is a country that does not need to be poor."[2] This is the righteous anger that lit a fire in my friend. He could see the untapped resources in the environment, but as he would soon discover, he and his people had long been overlooking the most important natural resource on the continent, a precious treasure-store that had long been largely ignored by the people of Africa and of the world—one that could change the whole outlook of previously depressed places.

With a heart to right wrongs in the world, Shiferaw pursued

justice as a career. He studied at Columbia University School of Law in the United States and went on to serve as Minister of Justice in the Ethiopian government. Finally, he founded a prosperous law firm in Addis Ababa. Then one day a man walked through the door of Shiferaw's law firm with a packet of papers in his hand. As he handed the pages of Ethiopian legalese to Shiferaw to translate, he told him his desire to bring his nonprofit, an organization that was already nourishing and nurturing children in other nations around the world, to the country. That organization was none other than Compassion International. As Shiferaw got to know this Compassion International representative, he thought back on the life-giving way his mother had parented him and how that had led him to try big things.

As he talked with this gentleman, Shiferaw began to believe that children could be Africa's greatest resource. Now if he could figure out how to nurture that resource instead of allowing it to be abused or exploited, as so often happened with valuable resources, then why wouldn't positive change occur across the entire continent? As he considered his own fulfilling childhood and the life-giving work of this nonprofit, something stirred inside him. The Lord spoke first to Shiferaw's wife, impressing on her that Shiferaw should close the law firm and join efforts with Compassion International. *Close the law firm? After all it had taken to get to this point?* he wondered. Hesitant, he prayed with her, thinking that the idea would be put to rest and that they could go on as before. But the closer Shiferaw put his ear to the heart of the Lord, the louder he heard it beating for children. Still, Shiferaw resisted. "Starting a new thing has its own joys," he says, "but can also be very taxing."[3] It didn't take long for him to agree that his wife had heard the Lord correctly. There was no use in running from the calling. As Psalm 139:7 says, "Where shall I go from your Spirit? Or where shall I flee from your presence?" Shiferaw said, "God spoke to me very clearly. To have my peace, I said yes."[4]

Shiferaw was known in his nation for his keen mind and wisdom in law. He greatly enjoyed his work and his position of influence. But God had in mind a whole different area of influence for him. Just as God had moved my friends Iman Santoso and Alex Philip out from the medical profession, He was now calling Shiferaw Michael out from the field of law. As it turns out, our Lord calls not only humble fishermen to His school of discipleship, but doctors and lawyers, too.

And so Shiferaw stepped away from the desks and doorframes of the law firm that had his name on it, and stepped forward as the founding leader of Compassion International in Ethiopia. There are very few countries he has not stepped foot in for the cause of children since that day. As Shiferaw served with Compassion International and as Justice Minister in Ethiopia, he saw time and again how the attitudes in the core of society impacted the development of the nation's children and therefore decided the nation's future.

THE ORIGINAL CELL OF SOCIAL LIFE

Over the years, from our days in war-torn El Salvador to our visits to the gateway cities of the 10/40 Window, Doris and I have taken part in many community transformations. But through it all, we have never taken for granted that our first priority must be to stay grounded in the smallest circle of influence the Lord has entrusted to us—our own family. Our highest priority when our children were under our roof was to love them through their many growing pains and root them in Scripture, prayer, and the Great Commission.

I love the way Geordon Rendle, former president of Youth for Christ International, and his wife, Marilyn, describe their life mission: "to nurture a family and impact a generation."[5] It starts with the family, this small, ultra-local entity at the microlevel of day-to-day interactions between members of a shared household. For all of the needs in the world, we cannot neglect the ones tugging at our shirttails.

As our four children—Jeannine, Stephanie, Naomi, and Daniel—grew up, we started each day with the simple nourishment of Bible reading and conversation while we ate breakfast together. In the evenings, we would read a good book aloud, like a book from The Chronicles of Narnia. As the days rolled on and our kids became teenagers, Doris and I took time to frequently meet one on one with each of our children throughout this pivotal time. I even had opportunities to include each of them on international ministry trips.

It's a joy to see our now-adult children rearing their own children, each dedicating their family to God's Word and prayer in living daily life together. But Doris and I are by no means finished with our work. We have the great joy of connecting on an ongoing basis with our older grandchildren, discipling this new generation in our own family. As I teach my grandchildren the methods of personal Bible study, they come back to me with fresh insights, things I hadn't noticed in all my years of studying Scripture. My oldest grandchild, twenty-one-year-old Gabriella, and I frequently connect via video chat while she is studying in Germany. We have been working our way through the book of John, paragraph by paragraph. God's Word fuels her as she meets weekly with one particular classmate and friend, a Syrian refugee, to share recipes, cook together, and talk about their faith. As we disciple her, she is pouring into others. What a privilege to lead and guide our little followers while they are still looking to us.

I like the way the Catholic Catechism puts it:

> The family is the *original cell of social life*. It is the natural society in which husband and wife are called to give themselves in love and in the gift of life. Authority, stability, and a life of relationships within the family constitute the foundations for freedom, security, and fraternity within society. The family is the community in which, from childhood, one can learn moral values, begin to honor God, and make good use of freedom. Family life is an initiation into life in society.[6]

There is no better framework than the family for ongoing discipleship. Shiferaw says, "The family is the arena where the entire range of human experiences takes place. Hence, by equipping, empowering and encouraging the family to perform its role in raising children according to God's ways, children receive a heritage that significantly strengthens children's ministry in the church."[7]

With this vision in mind, a few years after founding Compassion International in Ethiopia, Shiferaw stepped further into the task of turning the heart of his people toward the children of Africa. To do this, he founded the Child Development Training and Research Center, an institute that educates children's workers in Africa—Sunday school teachers, staff serving in orphanages, and those working for child-focused nonprofits like World Vision and Compassion. But he drills deeper to the inner circle of the child, to the family unit, the institution that will have the greatest impact on the well-being of that child. Using small changes to impact a big issue, he helps parents resist negative cultural norms and transform their families and society, starting with themselves.

NO MORE LEFTOVERS

In Shiferaw's culture, especially in the rural areas of Ethiopia, children are often treated as afterthoughts. Children don't sit and eat with their parents at the dinner table. Perhaps because of scarcity of food and resources, parents tend to eat first, and then whatever remains after they are filled goes to the children. In founding the Child Development Training and Research Center in Ethiopia, Shiferaw hoped to challenge the men and women in his workshops with something as simple as initiating family dinner. Starting with this daily ritual, he would "heat the heart and mind" of parents and other caregivers so they would be primed to have their worldview shifted.[8] He wanted them to understand and care about the plight of children, get a vision for the potential of children, appreciate the personhood of the child, and see their children not as burdens, but as the precious resource that they are. Shiferaw's training has challenged parents, teachers, and caregivers to view the child in front of them like Shiferaw's mother saw her children.

Shiferaw sees his work as preparing the way for transformation in the lives of families, the church, and society as a whole, echoing the ministry of John the Baptist, "to turn the hearts of the parents to their children and the disobedient to the wisdom of the righteous—to make ready a people prepared for the Lord" (Luke 1:17 NIV). In a beautiful display of repentance and grace, mothers and fathers, both Christian and non-Christian, have been so moved by the child development workshops at the institute that they have hardly been able to wait until the training is finished to make amends with their children. "Many have gone back to their homes, asked their children for forgiveness, embraced and hugged them, and invited them to eat at the table," says Shiferaw.[9]

After another one of Shiferaw's training sessions, one young man became so burdened for the overlooked children in his church that he went home and started doing some math. He counted the number of children in the congregation, counted the number of church members, and then shared his vision with the adults in the congregation. All in agreement, the young man assigned five children to every adult church member. "There would be no orphan child, not even a spiritual orphan," Shiferaw said, referring to those children whose parents are at home physically yet neglect to actively care for their children.[10]

The adults in that church have committed to pray for each of the five children under their care, and to show them attention and affection with a pat on the back or even helping with grooming, such as braiding a child's hair. "It's a sponsorship of love. It's just amazing. The church has grown. It has become a love-filled church," Shiferaw said.[11]

WATERS YOU WILL NEVER GET BACK

Around the turn of the millennium, a few years before Shiferaw and I met, the Transform World movement began. As my friends and I considered what it would take to truly see transformation in communities worldwide, and while Shiferaw was busy doing his work in Ethiopia unbeknownst to me, I found myself thinking similar thoughts about the untapped potential of children. I had raised my children and sent them out like arrows into the world, but I couldn't steer my mind from the generation after them. I couldn't stop thinking of that segment of society that seemed to be an afterthought in the countries of the 10/40 Window, the segment of society that has so often been seen as a burden instead of a blessing, the segment of society that Jesus sees as especially equipped to follow His lead and bless the world.

I shared with Doris and our son, Daniel, in 2001 that I sensed God was revealing something about the importance of children in the transformation of these underdeveloped areas of the world, and in the world as a whole. A few years later, at a Transform World event hosted with Tim Keller and others, I had the great pleasure of meeting and sharing this vision with Nam Soo Kim, the soft-spoken Korean pastor from the New York City area whom you met in the last chapter.

Upon my arrival at Promise Church in New York in December 2008, Nam Soo Kim looked at me and said, "I have been waiting for you." Doris did a double take, wondering what he might mean. Nam Soo Kim explained that for the past ten years, he had been holding on to a vision for the world's children. Promise Church's ministries were already stepping out to bless children locally in their neighborhood through Power House and internationally through supporting children in schools in Latin America. Still, Nam Soo Kim was awaiting the birth of a global movement with a heart for children. He said, "Luis, this is my burden. Would you join me in seeing this vision fulfilled?" This shared vision confirmed the work that God had been doing in my own heart. We gave each other a hearty handshake, a symbol of newfound friendship and a mutual commitment to a global children's movement. It was a true yes effect moment.

Soon after that, I did what we had done before the 10/40 Window concept had emerged. I began asking questions, researching, and mapping out ideas to bring this demographic and concept to the forefront. In the process of writing a book about the issue and considering the invaluable work of Dr. Dan Brewster, an expert in holistic child development and theology, the "4/14 Window" moniker emerged. Soon we began planning a 4/14 Global Summit, to be hosted by Promise Church. Former Compassion International Director for Asia, Dr. Bambang Budijanto, agreed to chair the emerging 4/14 Movement Steering Committee, bringing vital perspective and leadership with him.

Unlike the 10/40 Window, which is a geographic window of latitude and longitude, the 4/14 Window is a demographic one, a window of time that opens up in every person between the ages of four and fourteen. Children age fifteen and under make up a whopping one-third of the world's population. In the countries of the 10/40 Window, the most resource-deprived and gospel-deprived areas of the world, nearly half of the population fits within the 4/14 Window, this most formative decade in a child's life.[12]

But this age group isn't a standout just for the sheer number it contains. This age group is remarkable because they possess a special openness that grown-ups just don't have. Surveys of believers on every continent from every background show that the majority of those who choose to follow Christ do so before age eighteen, with 70 percent doing so between the ages of four and fourteen.[13] Remarkably, 70 percent of those are led to faith by their own peers.[14] Yet the average church puts only 3 percent of its resources toward reaching this particular demographic.[15]

When God struck a match in our hearts and gave us a vision for reaching children, Nam Soo Kim combed the historical documents from a hundred years of international missionary conventions looking for the ministry initiatives of those who had come before. In all the proclamations and declarations, he found little mention of children. He shook his head at the thought of the sinister regimes of the world that "invest in children for the next generation and the next and the next after that. They see five hundred years ahead. But the Christian church forgets everything. They only think about the building, their projects, their denomination. They only see themselves, their own generation."[16] Jesus' own words from Matthew 19:14 (NIV) have been echoing in our hearts: "Let the little children come to me, and do not hinder them, for the kingdom of heaven belongs to such as these." Perhaps the church had not directly hindered them, but had we truly helped either? If the church ignores the core work of making disciples during this vital time and falls instead for materialism, consumerism, and the prosperity gospel, each congregation working to achieve megachurch status, in forty to fifty years they will crumble to nothing. "If they go wrong at the bottom," Nam Soo Kim says of the modern church, "they have to go all the way back. If they lose the children, they lose everything."[17]

Over the last twenty-five years, the church has gone great distances to bless the nations of the 10/40 Window. We have drilled wells for clean water. We have translated Bibles into tribal languages. We have built churches in places where Christ was once unknown. We have worked with Jesus and each other to do big things. But now we must go smaller. We must stoop low to engage with the children among us. Whether you look at the abortion statistics in developed nations or the child abandonment statistics in developing countries, it is clear that too many adults see children as expendable or insignificant.

As Shiferaw Michael says, "If you don't make use of the early years of life, they are like a river that has flowed, whose waters you will never get back."[18] Let it not be so for the church. As we in the 4/14 Movement say, "Where the world sees immaturity and foolishness, God sees windows, tender open hearts responsive to His leading. . . . Today, we have an amazing opportunity to bring God's love to millions of open windows."[19]

A NEW KIND OF PLAYGROUND

While the most lasting transformation comes through face-to-face mentorship, we must also be willing to reach out to children beyond our homes, our own local churches, and our neighborhoods. For better or worse, the Internet is this generation's playground. LaReau Anderson, a friend of the 4/14 Movement, says, "We see even in the poorest of the poor communities, the choice being made to buy a cellphone instead of buying food. That's the reality. Our desire for connectedness is so key. It's just a part of our human DNA. We want to be connected."[20]

We may set boundaries in our own homes to limit online connection in favor of face-to-face connection, but statistics show that other families are spending a significant amount of their waking hours on some kind of device. Common Sense Media reported that in 2013, children ages five to eight spent more than two hours a day on screen time, eight- to twelve-year-olds use entertainment media for an average of six hours daily, and thirteen to eighteen year-olds spend about nine hours on entertainment media.[21]

Certainly for the well-being of children and families, parents should limit screen time for both themselves and their children. They should lay down very clear boundaries to ensure good mental development, spiritual and emotional health, and social and physical safety. For this, Common Sense Media provides some great resources for developing a family agreement, and discerning what types of media are more concerning than others. There is much to be leery of on the Internet, but we don't want to abstain from it altogether. We want to use the tools in front of us without letting them use us.

Scripture says believers are like salt and light, bringing flavor and color to our surroundings. "You are the light of the world," Jesus says. "A town built on a hill cannot be hidden. Neither do people light a lamp and put it under a bowl. Instead they put it on its stand, and it gives light to everyone in the house. In the same way, let your light shine before others, that they may see your good deeds and glorify your Father in heaven" (Matt. 5:14–16 NIV). If we withdraw completely from the Internet, who will provide the saltiness to help those online to "taste and see that the LORD is good" (Ps. 34:8)? If we snuff out our light, the digital world may become nothing but a wasteland of violence, pornography, social media arguments, and maybe a few funny cat videos. LaReau Anderson says,

> Whether we like it or not, this media is here to stay. This world that we're living in, this lightning fast Roman Road, as we might call it, is not going to go away. It's going to get faster. The influence is going to get stronger and deeper. And the more we can recognize that and the more we can come alongside and offer these positive alternatives in media and literature, the better it's going to be for the kids growing up in our world today. . . . So, we're trying to create resources that can help people connect, help them connect in really healthy ways, and engage in the world in a way that is honoring to God.[22]

Over the years, we've seen the development of many resources to do just that. One of those is The Story of Jesus app developed by Youth for Christ, which communicates the narrative of Jesus' life and His gift of redemption in an accessible way to digital natives. Another resource, the Bible App for Kids, developed in partnership with OneHope, allows children to explore the Bible in their generation's mode of interactive learning as they click on maps, thought bubbles, and other icons to discover the story of Scripture. It is currently available in fourteen languages with at least ten more in the works. Putting this far-reaching technology to use gives children and families access to the nourishing Word of God in the venue where many of their waking hours are spent.

It is vital that we step out into the virtual neighborhood and reach people where they are. Though technology often distracts from our most nourishing in-person relationships, and though some of its content can compromise users' emotional and spiritual health, the tools of technology can be used to introduce all peoples, including the next generation, to the wholesome, holistic, life-giving message of Jesus. Evil is trying to get its screen time, but that's not where the story ends. Just as I witnessed God use the emerging tools of mapping technology to help us center on the 10/40 Window in 1989, we are seeing a great dispersion of the gospel through the Internet in this day and age. As the World Wide Web truly becomes worldwide, so does our reach.

KINESTHETIC FAITH

As we lead our followers, we need to be willing to do much more than just provide for children's daily needs and provide enough entertainment to keep them out of our hair. And we must do more than just give them a good foundation in the Word of God. We must also help them engage the natural skills they've been given, build up strong character, and push off from the starting block to exercise their faith.

When I was growing up, my father encouraged us kids to get involved in sports, not because he was one of those overly competitive parents who wanted to live vicariously through his children, but because he knew that in sports, you learn how to play on a team. He wanted us to practice doing our part and letting others do theirs. He wanted us to work hard. He wanted us to grow from our disappointments and maintain a learning posture, ready to be coached on how to improve our approach. It is vital that children have the chance to put their faith in motion, to apply what they have learned from being rooted in Scripture and from watching our steps of faith.

Dr. William Damon, one of the world's leading scholars on human development, cautions us not to assume that our kids need to veg out in front of the television for a good portion of every day. He urges parents to consider how to engage their children in worthwhile endeavors, something young people can be proud of and find meaning in. He warns us not to overlook the child's innate desire to be a change agent in the world:

> In systematically underestimating the child's capabilities, we are limiting the child's potential for growth. In withholding from children the expectation to serve others as well as the expectation to care for themselves, we are preventing them from acquiring a sense of social and personal responsibility. We are leaving the child to dwell on nothing more noble than gratifying the self's moment-by-moment inclinations. In the end, this orientation is a particularly unsatisfying form of self-centeredness, because it creates a focus on a personal self that has no special skills or valued services to offer anyone else. Paradoxically, by giving the child purposes that go beyond the self, an orientation to service results in a more secure belief in oneself.[23]

Children are not just a mission field; they are mission agents. Unless we want to stunt their growth, we must open our hands and let each child embark on his or her own journey of faith and service.

In Scripture, we see countless examples of God interacting with and inviting children to take action in response to their circumstance, to join God in starting a chain reaction. We see Miriam, who watched over her baby brother, Moses, on the banks of the Nile. When Pharaoh's daughter found Moses, she coordinated for him to be nursed by his own biological mother who would teach him the ways of the Lord until his days in the palace. We see Samuel—dedicated in service to God by his mother, Hannah, even before he was conceived—who heard the voice of God in the temple, even when the grown-up priest did not. We see the young David taking down Israel's loud-mouthed enemy, Goliath, with a simple sling. We see a young servant girl speaking up about her faith in God and leading Namaan, commander of the Syrian army, to find healing. We see King Josiah, who began his reign at age eight, cleansing the temple of false idols and leading his nation to repent and recommit themselves to the Lord.

In the New Testament, we see the boy with five loaves and two fish who teams up with Jesus to feed five thousand people. We see Jesus Himself who entered the temple at age twelve to discuss Scripture with the scribes. And we see adult Jesus gathering the children to sit with him. Let us not be like the disciples who hindered the children from interacting with Jesus.

Dr. Bambang Budijanto says, "From ages 1–5, children learn by what is done to them. From ages 6–10, they learn by what they are shown by others. But ages 11–18, young people learn by what they DO. This is why we are calling on all young people to DO—to invest in the next generation and make disciples."[24]

Jesus put no prerequisites on the Great Commission. His salvation is not just for those old enough to vote. We believe that around age eleven, children are developmentally able to both understand and respond to the assignment Jesus gave us to go and make disciples. From this understanding, an initiative called Nurturer has emerged within the older half of the 4/14 Window. In sync with Jesus' words, Nurturer is a call for every person in the church age eleven and up to take part in sharing the story of Jesus and in training people in a life of faith. Older brothers and sisters can study the Bible with their siblings. Young people can help classmates with difficult coursework and share how they lean on the Lord in times of stress. Children can even speak truth and grace into the lives of the adults around them. No matter our age, we grow by helping others grow.[25]

THE KID PREACHER

When Peter addressed the crowds in Jerusalem on the Day of Pentecost, he said, "In the last days, God says, I will pour out my Spirit on all people. Your sons and daughters will prophesy, your young men will see visions, your old men will dream dreams" (Acts 2:17 NIV). Indeed, we see God raising up children today to join us as ambassadors of His goodness in the world.

A few years back, as God was lining up so many people from all over the world with a fresh eagerness for connecting with 4/14ers, my friend Ricardo Luna called his friend Andres Castelazo, vice president of the Evangelical Alliance in Mexico. He told him that on his next trip to Mexico, he wanted to gather ten to twelve pastors with whom he could share the vision of the 4/14 Window to see what God might do. "I gave him two months' notice," Ricardo said, "and to make a long story short, when I walked into the meeting, there were 1,214 pastors waiting for me. I asked for twelve. I got twelve hundred."[26] Clearly, God was up to something as this many pastors gathered openly in Chiapas, Mexico, a region ripe with religious tension.

For many years, Chiapas had been like Russia in the Cold War. You could not share the gospel. You could not sing a Christian song. You could not build a church. One martyr had even been scalped. One young lady who had come to Christ through signs and wonders was shot nineteen times. Yet somehow she didn't die. Neither did the church.

Ricardo watched that day as Andres Castelazo's four-year-old grandson, Israel, gave a devotional message in front of twelve hundred pastors in Chiapas. The boy didn't know how to read, but had been listening to Bible stories since the day he was born. During the meeting, he told the story of David and Goliath, discerning its deeper meaning and preaching its principles to the pastors and community leaders in the room. As he ended, he said, "Some of you are thinking about your Goliath. Yes, that person, that situation standing before you. And what God did with David, today Jesus can do with you. If you turn your Goliath over to Jesus, you can watch him fall. That's the God we serve."[27]

As the boy Israel sat down, Ricardo heard a strange sound coming from the chair next to him where the minister of religion for Chiapas was seated. This government official, this man who carried the heavy responsibility of trying to end the violence in his conflicted community, a hardened, unbelieving man, began to sob. "Nobody can touch this guy, but the Lord used a four-year-old kid to break through," Ricardo said, "I say if God wants to do that, we should let Him."[28]

As my co-laborer in the ministry John Hur put it, "Our children need to be discipled to disciple all the nations." He further states, "So far, they were just the object of our mission. But now we declare that they are our partners in mission."[29] John uses the idea of an arrow to describe the generational cooperation that it takes to launch the message of Jesus into all the earth. The arrowhead, he says, represents the child, who must be sharp and streamlined, ready to soar. The shaft of the arrow represents the parents, who must give the child moral fiber and direction. The feathers of the arrow represent the grandparents, who offer balance and stability from many years of growing in faith.[30]

Geordon Rendle, former president of Youth for Christ International, says,

> God is raising up new generational leaders, but that doesn't mean he discards the old ones. We always challenge the younger generation to honor the older. The reverse is also true. The older generation needs to honor the younger ones by releasing roles, responsibilities, and titles. Step aside, but don't step away.[31]

We need to mobilize older generations to turn their attention to the younger generation, to network, pool resources, provide training, and cheer our 4/14ers on as they take up the mantle of ministry where they are now.

HIS WORKMANSHIP

What children has God placed in your family, your circle of friends, or your church? How might you come alongside and bless them? I invite you to take part in the 4/14 Movement right where you are by engaging, protecting, establishing, and empowering the children in your life to take their rightful place in God's transformational work in the world. In this busy day and age, kids are often overlooked and yearn for personal attention, connection, and guidance from a caring adult. How might you make yourself more accessible and attentive for the children around you? Get less busy. Become more observant. The simple act of asking questions about a child's interests can speak volumes in communicating your care for them. Some kids are in more dire situations and need to be rescued from dangerous influences or depression and given a safe place to recover and grow. With all that these kids face, it is also vital in the developmental years between the ages of four to fourteen to give children a spiritual foundation, rooting them in a relationship with Christ through prayer and study of His Word. In the midst of daily routines or more difficult challenges, as you make yourself available to the kids in your circle, you will find teachable moments when a child is especially open to deeper conversation. And as they grow, you can give them more and more independent opportunities to take part in sharing Jesus with those around them.

I had the incredible opportunity not only to take my children on my assignments around the world, but to send them into the world when they were ready. Altogether, as teenagers and young adults, my children served on seventeen short-term international mission teams without me. After spending many years of childhood on the mission field in El Salvador and meeting the internationals who visited our home over the years, our oldest daughter, Jeannine, says that the seeds of mission were planted deep into her heart. "I was certain that life would not have its full meaning without me giving of myself to serve God on His mission," she says of her teen years. She says her experience on mission "solidified deep compassion for a world where my peers did not have the opportunities and freedoms that I had, where women didn't have a say, and yet their work was burdensome, even stifling to their well-being. My perspective would never be the same. My worldview had grown beyond the Western world and I had found a purpose for existence beyond myself and my average teen mindset."

Our second daughter, Stephanie, tells me it was during a summer in Egypt that her faith truly became her own. As she saw God's work in the world with her own eyes, she came to trust Him more deeply. It was a challenge for her to return to public school when the school year started. She had that out-of-place feeling, trying to be relevant to her peers with the realities they face, having witnessed people suffering in other parts of the world, those just trying to survive. "I was like a fish swimming against the current," she said, "There were many times I was ridiculed and made fun of for my faith. I was isolated and felt very lonely at times." But being rooted in Scripture, she clung to the promise that Jesus would never leave her nor forsake her (see Heb. 13:5). She affirmed that promise to be true as we released her to test the tenets of her faith out in the world. "I knew I was not alone," she said, "Just as Jesus proved to be near during my mission trips, He was so very close, walking the hallways of my school with me."

Naomi, our third daughter, also remarks that serving on short-term mission trips during her summer vacations as a youth helped her get through her junior high and high school years. It was an exercise in faith for her to raise the necessary financial support and to step out to serve without our family. Each time she ventured out to be involved in God's work in the world, she returned with amazing mission field stories and testimonies.

Our son, Daniel, found his mission experiences to be a very important part of his development as well. He worshiped alongside believers who spoke other languages and saw the church from a non-Western perspective.

As Doris and I released each of our children to experience God for themselves and to impact the world in their own way, they exercised their faith and grew up to be people of empathy and action. It has been the great joy of our lives to cheer them on as they each run their own race, saying yes to the opportunities God places before them and watching new ones open up.

Children—they are fearfully and wonderfully made, they are born to us with their own personality traits, a special knack for particular activities, and a curiosity about the world around them. We have the privilege of walking alongside our children, helping them to grow in the Lord and say yes themselves to the invitations God is extending them. As we commit them to Jesus and co-labor with Him, we can marvel as year by year, layer by layer, He transforms them into His workmanship, created in Christ Jesus for good works (Eph. 2:10).

Choose Your Adventure

When our children were growing up, a new type of reading material began to appear on library and bookstore shelves, offering a fresh way for young readers of that era to experience a story line. Through these books, readers went from being observers to participants. As a kid cracked open a book in the *Choose Your Own Adventure* series, he or she would take on the role of the main character. As one event led to another, the reader would come to a turning point, and have the opportunity to choose the way he or she would go, turning to one page or another to follow a particular path. Upon getting lost in a cave as night approaches, the reader could choose to try to go back home by turning to one page, or to camp out overnight in the cave by turning to another page. Stuck in the snowy mountains, the reader could choose to follow a set of footprints or stay near a crashed rescue copter and hope help would come. Each choice had its own corresponding sequence of events.

For all time, God has been laying out an invitation, a choice before His people. Deuteronomy 30:19–20 (NIV) says, "I have set before you life and death, blessings and curses. Now choose life, so that you and your children may live and that you may love the LORD your God, listen to his voice, and hold fast to him. For the LORD is your life."

In Matthew 19, just after Jesus took the children in His arms and blessed them, saying, "The kingdom of God belongs to such as these," a man, known as the rich young ruler, came to him and fell on his knees before Jesus. "Teacher, what good deed must I do to have eternal life?" he asked.

Jesus replied, ". . . If you would enter life, keep the commandments."

"Which ones?" the man asked, undoubtedly running through the memorized list in his head.

Jesus listed off six commandments: "You shall not murder, You shall not commit adultery, You shall not steal, You shall not bear false witness, Honor your father and mother, and, You shall love your neighbor as yourself."

Simple enough. He had kept all of these commandments since his youth, at least in his own estimation. Jesus could undoubtedly see the calculations working out behind this man's eyes. He could see the insecurity that had propelled this man to come kneeling and asking questions. Jesus had compassion on this man who was entrenched in a maxed out, tight-fisted way of life. For all the learning, for all the possessions, for all the status, for all the earthly security, this man remained unsettled.

"Jesus looked at him and loved him," Mark says in his account. Out of His love for him, Jesus pointed him to the heart of the issue. "One thing you lack," Jesus continued. "Go, sell everything you have and give to the poor, and you will have treasure in heaven. Then come, follow me" (Mark 10:21 NIV).

This man, worried about his eternal destiny, had been un-aware that he could start living his eternal life here on earth even now, that he could transfer his citizenship to heaven and start living the abundant life before his dying day. Maybe he had felt the itch in his spirit, instinctively knowing: "No one can serve two masters. Either you will hate the one and love the other, or you will be devoted to the one and despise the other. You cannot serve both God and money" (Matt. 6:24 NIV). His house and hands were full, but his soul felt empty. He had a choice to make. He could say yes and accept Jesus' very special invitation to give up "what he cannot keep to gain what he cannot lose," as missionary Jim Elliot famously put it.[1] Or he could continue letting his possessions possess him. Sell your shackles, Jesus suggested. Come live free with Me, He offered.

This man had a choice to make, and if you haven't heard this story before, you might assume he'd choose to follow Jesus. But in Mark 10:22, we read a haunting phrase: "At this the man's face fell. He went away sad, because he had great wealth" (NIV). He could have joined Jesus and walked free. But he went away. And he went away *sad*. Back to the many cares of his many things. Back to his questions, uncertainty, and insecurity. Back to the ceaseless striving. Back to the ball and chain of worldly treasure. Back to everlasting dissatisfaction. Back to watching, wondering, worrying. And away from abundant life on the dusty path of adventure. He went away. He went away sad.

With the invitation to follow Jesus right in front of him, the rich man held on to other allegiances, other cares. How would you respond to that invitation? Mark 4:18–19 says, "Still others, like seed sown among thorns, hear the word; but the worries of this life, the deceitfulness of wealth and the desires for other things come in and choke the word, making it unfruitful" (NIV). Jesus had given this man the words of life, the key to unlock the shackles of materialism, consumerism, status, and all the weight of the world. But he would not turn the key. He would remain a slave to wealth and its worries.

Matthew 6:33 says, "But seek first the kingdom of God and his righteousness, and all these things will be added to you." Certainly Jesus doesn't ask an all-encompassing vow of poverty from every person. But worldly goods were the things keeping this particular person from embracing adventure with Jesus. Could this or something else, perhaps, be keeping you from saying yes to Jesus?

PECULIAR PEOPLE, PIVOTAL MOMENTS

It is a frightening prospect to say no, to think that you could turn the page and so soon discover that you've chosen the less fulfilling way and missed out on participating in a movement of God, whether on a grand or small scale.

In the Old Testament, Esther, the Jewish girl turned Persian queen, faced the dilemma of whether she should approach her intimidating husband, King Xerxes, reveal her hidden identity as a Jew, and ask him to halt his plan to destroy her people. As a person living between cultures, what we sometimes call a third-culture person, she had a unique position of influence. With a heart for her people, an understanding of the social and political climate in which they lived, and a unique relationship with the leader of the land, she had an opportunity and a responsibility before her. But would she risk her safety and say yes?

At this pivotal moment, Esther's cousin Mordecai counseled her. "For if you remain silent at this time," he said, "relief and deliverance for the Jews will arise from another place, but you and your father's family will perish. And who knows but that you have come to your royal position for such a time as this?" (Est. 4:14 NIV). Esther's heart stirred for her people. She urged them to pray. She called for a fast. And then she stepped forward to change history. God can allow His plans to be carried out one way or another, but we have a choice as to whether we get involved and do our part or whether we will forfeit the opportunity and sit on the sidelines.

Like Queen Esther, we followers of Jesus often find ourselves living between two cultures. We are citizens of our home nations, yet our ultimate citizenship is in heaven. It may feel a little uncomfortable at times, but being a third-culture person allows unique opportunities for understanding and impacting the situations around us. Third-culture people may, like me, feel as if they belong everywhere and nowhere at the same time. "Instinctively, we don't see borders," says my friend Geordon Rendle, who calls himself a "raving" third-culture kid, having spent a significant part of his youth in a culture other than the one that he and his family called home. "We see possibilities that are above and beyond borders," he says. "Third-culture kids should be the prototype of kingdom citizens."[2]

The world today is in dire need of people who see beyond borders, who see possibility instead of limits, who will step out of the status quo, go against the flow, and let God use them as agents of redemption, reconciliation, and transformation.

In the second century AD, in the *Epistle to Diognetus*, an anonymous follower of Jesus wrote about these intriguing people dispersed in so many cultures of the known world, people who spoke the language and dressed as their fellow citizens but lived from an uncommon set of values:

> For the Christians are distinguished from other men neither
> by country, nor language, nor the customs which they ob-
> serve. For they neither inhabit cities of their own, nor employ
> a peculiar form of speech, nor lead a life which is marked
> out by any singularity. . . . But, inhabiting Greek as well as
> barbarian cities . . . and following the customs of the natives
> in respect to clothing, food, and the rest of their ordinary
> conduct, they display to us their wonderful and confessedly
> striking method of life. They dwell in their own countries, but
> simply as [resident aliens]. As citizens, they share in all things
> with others, and yet endure all things as if foreigners. Every
> foreign land is to them as their native country, and every
> land of their birth as a land of strangers. They marry . . . they
> [have] children; but they do not destroy their offspring. They
> have a common table, but not a common bed. They are in
> the flesh, but they do not live after the flesh. They pass their
> days on earth, but they are citizens of heaven. They obey the
> prescribed laws, and at the same time surpass the laws by their
> lives. They love all men, and are persecuted by all. . . . They
> are poor, yet make many rich; they are in lack of all things,
> and yet abound in all. . . . They are reviled, and bless; they are
> insulted, and repay the insult with honour; they do good, yet
> are punished as evil-doers. . . . They are assailed by the Jews
> as foreigners, and are persecuted by the Greeks; yet those who

hate them are unable to assign any reason for their hatred. To sum up all in one word—what the soul is in the body, that are Christians in the world."[3]

Imagine how our communities could be impacted by a witness like this today. It's easy to see that these second-century believers were the spiritual descendants of the disciples of Jesus. The disciples, in stark contrast to the rich young ruler, followed Jesus' instructions to live simply, taking "no bag, no bread, no money, no extra shirt" as they practiced their faith, going from village to village to preach the good news and heal the sick (Luke 9:3 NIV). After Jesus' crucifixion, resurrection, and ascension, these disciples were found joyfully sharing the invitation of Jesus even in places where it wasn't well-received.

One day, the high priest in town, who was not a fan of the gospel, had the apostles arrested and thrown in jail. "But during the night an angel of the Lord opened the doors of the jail and brought them out" (Acts 5:19 NIV). The angel instructed them to go and preach in the temple courts. They accepted the challenge and started preaching at daybreak. In the morning, when the authorities arrived at the jail and found the doors securely locked with guards keeping watch over empty jail cells, "the captain of the temple guard and the chief priests were at a loss" (Acts 5:24 NIV).

The apostles were no passive observers. They were right in the thick of God's riveting story line, watching Him work, stepping out when He said to step out, and accepting His invitation to speak grace and truth in the public arena. When the authorities brought the followers of Jesus before the council again, they punished them and commanded them not to speak in the name of Jesus. But when you've been up close and personal with the One who opens tombs and prison doors, you see things a little differently. Unlike the rich young ruler who walked away sad, the apostles of Jesus "left . . . rejoicing that they were counted worthy to suffer dishonor for the name" of Jesus (Acts 5:41). For the love of God and their fellow human beings, these courageous followers of Jesus would leave the status quo and blaze the trail of faith with joy.

Compared to our modern way of life, the possessions and lifestyle of the rich young ruler may actually seem modest. Many of us live with overabundance, not only of material possessions, wealth, and status, but an overabundance of requests, comments, tweets, Facebook likes, and information. We are held down by a multiplicity of shackles, and we must ask ourselves if we would give them up if we had to—and perhaps more importantly, even if we don't have to. We could very well be holding on to things that are actually holding us back. Our over-connectedness may be causing us to be under-effective. We may indeed be suffering from compassion fatigue. But I invite you to push through all that and reflect for a minute on what you've discovered by meeting the adventurers in this book.

PART OF THE STORY

As we've traveled through the most needy places of the world in these pages, through garbage dump neighborhoods, refugee camps, and war zones, I hope you've been able to feel the plight of the widow, orphan, poor, and weary, and that you've seen them as more than social issues or statistics. I hope that as you've walked through the stories in this book, you've felt the cement around your own heart begin to crack and fall away.

Once upon a time, mission strategists called that band of nations paralyzed by poverty and blocked from the transforming power of the gospel the "Resistant Belt." But God helped us see that Resistant Belt in a whole new way, as a window of opportunity, the 10/40 Window. My hope is that God is doing something similar in you, that He is helping you find those areas of resistance in yourself and transforming them into something that lets in the light.

In that most needy section of the world, people had long been crushed under the weight of crumbling infrastructures that deprived citizens of clean water, nutrition, adequate shelter, and proper medical treatment. They've long been stifled by totalitarian governments that persecute the church and restrict education and work opportunities. But over the decades, as Jesus' followers have prayed and visited or moved their residence to be fully present with the people in the hardest hit areas of the world, we have seen pockets of God's kingdom springing up all over. A global chain reaction indeed!

Maybe when you look at the images of bloodshed and poverty on your television or tablet, you feel stunned. You see the weary people in your neighborhood and you sigh. You care, of course, but you feel ill-equipped to do anything about it. Each time you see another image or another person, you turn away a little more quickly. The problems on your own to-do list and in your own home feel beyond your scope, let alone tackling the problems of the world. But there is a way through.

Do you want to change the way your heart beats? Then put

your treasure where you *want* your heart to be. Jesus said, "But store up for yourselves treasures in heaven, where moths and vermin do not destroy, and where thieves do not break in and steal. For where your treasure is, there your heart will be also" (Matt. 6:20–21 NIV). Invest your time, energy, and resources, even in some small way *before* you feel like it, and your attention will automatically be drawn to that need. Compassion and a renewed sense of momentum will come.

Maybe like the rich young ruler, you are being invited to loosen your grip on your belongings, or perhaps your sense of belonging in your corner of the world. Instinctively, you know there is something more to life than the way you're living right now. Your life is full, but full of what? The Lord is inviting you to step away from distractions and step toward the people, place, or predicament He's placed on your heart. He is inviting you to give and serve generously out of your plenty—or even your little. You don't have to wait until you feel like you have it all together, until your energy tank or bank account is full.

In the first chapter of this book, we considered Hebrews 12:1–2 and how those who have run the race of faith in times past are now cheering us on. Those who said yes are shouting for us to throw off anything that would hold us back from accepting the invitation before us. Day after day, year after year, century after century, time has rolled from where they were to where we are. All along, from era to era, the gospel has gone forth because of the obedience of faithful believers. Today we build on the work of the apostles, the early church, the church fathers, the Reformers, those in the wave of modern missions, and every believer in between. We have much to learn from those who've gone before, who've given their lives to take the gospel to the farthest reaches of the world. What a privilege it is to be able to carry on that work—wherever we are. Will you join with the generations before you and link arms with the ones who come after? Will you run with endurance the race marked out for you? No more acting as a distant observer. No more waiting for a better time. No more saying no. It's time to become part of the story. It's time to choose your own adventure. It's time to go forward rejoicing instead of going away sad. It's time to say yes. The options are before you. So what will it be? The world is waiting for your answer.

Notes

*Some names have been changed or shortened to protect individuals and their ministries.

Invitation 1: Follow Your Leaders

1. Libby Hill, *The Chicago River, A Natural and Unnatural History* (Chicago: Lake Claremont Press, 2000), 139–51.

2. "Unification: Enter the CER, CRT and Subway," *Chicago-L.org*, http://www.chicago-l.org/history/unification.html.

3. Ralph Winter, "Unreached Peoples and Beyond," *Lausanne Movement*, 1974, https://www.lausanne.org/images/content/users/80/ TeachingTools/A2_TheCongress.pptx.

4. "Let the Earth Hear His Voice," *Lausanne*, http://www2.wheaton .edu/bgc/archives/bulletin/bu0708.htm

Invitation 2: Open Your Heart

1. "2 YEAR OLD GIRL RAN OVER IN CHINA - Baby ignored by 18 Chinese left to die in street! Yue Yue," video, 2:06, 2011, https:// www.youtube.com/watch?v=SFjdMKJVkzQ.

2. Kevin Dolak, "Chinese Toddler's Hit and Run: Mother Praises Rescuer," *ABC News*, October 19, 2011, http://abcnews.go.com/ blogs/headlines/2011/10/chinese-toddlers-hit-and-run-mother-praises-rescuer/.

3. Malcolm Moore, "Chinese hit-and-run toddler dies," *The Telegraph*, October 21, 2011, http://www.telegraph.co.uk/news/worldnews/asia/china/8840381/Chinese-girl-run-over-by-a-car-dies.html.

4. Ibid.

5. James Strong, *Strong's Expanded Exhaustive Concordance of the Bible* (Nashville: Thomas Nelson, 2009), 4697.

6. Father Sama'an, Interview with Craig and Darcy Wiley (Macon, France, June 2014).

7. Ibid.

8. Steve Weber and Anita Deyneka, Interview with Craig and Darcy Wiley (Macon, France, June 2014).

9. Ibid.

10. Linda Grant, Interview with Craig and Darcy Wiley (Geneva, Switzerland, June 2014).

11. Ibid.

12. Ibid.

13. Lizzie Porter, "Syrian Baby Girl Pulled Alive from the Rubble Is Reunited with the Tearful Hero Who Touched the Hearts of Millions," *Daily Mail*, http://www.dailymail.co.uk/news/article-3823755/I-hold-Syrian-baby-girl-pulled-ALIVE-rubble-reunited-tearful-hero-touched-hearts-millions.html.

14. Lena Masri, "Rescue Worker Cries as He Pulls Baby Alive from Rubble in Syria," *ABC News*, http://abcnews.go.com/International/rescue-worker-cries-pulls-baby-alive-rubble-syria/story?id=42481818.

15. Linda Grant, Interview with Craig and Darcy Wiley.

Invitation 3: Fix Your Eyes

1. Father Sama'an, Interview with Craig and Darcy Wiley (Macon, France, June 2014).

2. Bishop Mattaos, *The Biography of Saint Samaan the Shoemaker, "The Tanner"* (Cairo, Egypt: Church of Saint Samaan the Tanner in Mokattam, 1994), 56, quoted in *The Bible in Africa: Transactions, Trajectories, and Trends* (Leiden, Netherlands: Brill, 2000), 114.

3. Father Sama'an, Interview with Craig and Darcy Wiley.

4. Iman and Lea Santoso, Interview with Craig and Darcy Wiley (Macon, France, June 2014).

5. "Country: Indonesia," *Joshua Project*, https://joshuaproject.net/countries/ID.

6. "Indonesia," *Operation World*, http://www.operationworld.org/indo.

7. Iman and Lea Santoso, Interview with Craig and Darcy Wiley.

8. Ibid.

9. Ibid.

10. Ibid.

11. Steve Weber and Anita Deyneka, Interview with Craig and Darcy Wiley (Macon, France, June 2014).

12. Ibid.

13. Ibid.

14. Ibid.

15. Ibid.

16. Ibid.

17. "Praying through the Window," *AD2000*, http://www.ad2000.org/adoption/ptwiii.htm.

18. "Gateway Cities," *AD2000*, http://ad2000.org.

19. Luis Bush, "Report on Calcutta," 7–8.

20. Luis Bush, "Catalysts of World Evangelization" (PhD diss., Fuller Theological Seminary, 2002).

21. Rick Wood, "Bethany World Prayer Center Reaches Its Goal," *Mission Frontiers*, http://www.missionfrontiers.org/issue/article/bethany-world-prayer-center-reaches-its-goal.

22. Iman and Lea Santoso, Interview with Craig and Darcy Wiley.

23. Sue and Fred Rowe, with Luis Bush, *Transform World 2020 Prayer response to the challenges we are facing, Reflections as of August 18, 2015 by TW 2020 Celebration Challenge facilitators.*

Invitation 4: Move Your Feet

1. C. S. Lewis, *The Four Loves* (New York: Harcourt, Brace, 1960), 89.

2. Servants to Asia's Urban Poor, "Who We Are," http://servantsasia.org/who-we-are/about/.

3. Henri Nouwen, *Compassion: A Reflection on the Christian Life* (New York: Doubleday, 1982), 25.

4. "Central to the Ethos of Servants," *Servants in Asia*, http://servants asia.org/who-we-are/principles/

5. Raineer and Mila Chu, Corrie DeBoer and Manila Team, Interview by Craig and Darcy Wiley (Geneva, Switzerland, June 2014).

6. Ibid.

7. Ibid.

8. Ibid.

9. Ibid.

10. Ibid.

11. Ibid.

12. Ezra and Anna Jin, Interview by Craig and Darcy Wiley (Macon, France, June 2014).

13. Ibid.

14. Ibid.

15. Ibid.

16. Jason Mandryk, *Operation World* (Colorado Springs: GMI, 2010), 215.

17. Ezra and Anna Jin, Interview by Craig and Darcy Wiley.

18. Ibid.

19. Tania Branigan, "Tenth Apparent Suicide at Foxconn iPhone Factory in China," *The Guardian*, http://www.theguardian.com/world/2010/may/27/foxconn-suicide-tenth-iphone-china.

20. Chao Deng, "China's Cutthroat School System Leads to Teen Suicides," *The Wall Street Journal*, http://blogs.wsj.com/chinarealtime/2014/05/15/chinas-cutthroat-school-system-leads-to-teen-suicides/.

21. Ezra and Anna Jin, Interview by Craig and Darcy Wiley.

22. Ibid.

23. Ibid.

24. Mandryk, *Operation World*, 215.

25. Calum MacLeod, "Child's Death Prompts China to Look at Morals," *USA Today*, http://usatoday30.usatoday.com/news/world/story/2011-10-27/chinese-child-death-questions-morals/50967924/1.

26. Ibid.

27. Ezra and Anna Jin, Interview by Craig and Darcy Wiley.

28. Nabil Salib and Scott Gillis, Interview by Craig and Darcy Wiley, June 2014.

29. "Overview of the Refugee Crisis in Europe," Doctors without Borders, accessed February 3, 2016, http://www.msf.org.uk/overview-of-the-refugee-crisis-in-europe.

30. David Stoop, *You Are What You Think* (Grand Rapids: Revell, 1996), 110.

31. Henry and Melvin Blackaby, *Experiencing the Spirit: The Power of Pentecost Every Day* (Colorado Springs: Multnomah, 2009), 17.

Invitation 5: Find Your People

1. Nabil Salib and Scott Gillis, Interview with Craig and Darcy Wiley (Geneva, Switzerland, June 2014).

2. Ibid.

3. Ibid.

4. Terry Dalrymple, email message to author, July 1, 2016.

5. John Warton, Interview by Craig and Darcy Wiley (Macon, France, June 2014).

6. Mohammed Ali, "The Link Between Unemployment and Terrorism," *TED*, https://www.ted.com/talks/mohamed_ali_the_link_between_unemployment_and_terrorism/transcript?language=en.

7. John Warton, Transform World Summit: Business Sphere, video, 6:55, https://vimeo.com/66698508.

8. Ibid.

9. C. Neal Johnson, *Business as Mission: A Comprehensive Guide to Theory and Practice* (Downers Grove, IL: IVP Academic, 2009), 70.

10. Ibid.

11. John Warton, Interview by Craig and Darcy Wiley.

12. Wael Salah Fahmi and Keith Sutton, "Cairo's Zabaleen Garbage Recyclers: Multi-Nationals' Takeover and State Relocation Plans," *Habitat International* 30, no. 4 (2006): 811. https://trashethnography.wikispaces.com/file/view/Cairo%27s+Zabaleen+garbage+recyclers,+Multi-Nationals%27+takeover+and+state+relocation+plans.pdf.

13. Ibid.

14. Father Sama'an, Interview by Craig and Darcy Wiley (Macon, France, June 2014).

15. "Fr. Samaan and Garbage City (Zabaleen) Part 1," video, 6:36, https://www.youtube.com/watch?v=e01d4OlTi_k.

16. Ibid.

17. Barbora Sajmovicova, "Zabbaleen - The Garbage Collectors," *Ethnologist*, http://ethnologist.info/2015/08/28/zabaleen-the-garbage-collectors/.

18. Alan Kadduri, "Turning Waste into Wealth with Cairo's Garbage People," *Your Middle East*, http://www.yourmiddleeast.com/culture/turning-waste-into-wealth-with-cairos-garbage-people-photos_31874.

19. Ibid.

20. Ibid.

21. "Zabbaleen: Trash Town. A whole community in Egypt that lives on rubbish," RT Documentary, video, 25:29, https://www.youtube.com/watch?v=D0s7WsoC528.

22. Fred De Sam Lazaro, "In Cairo's Trash City, School Teaches Reading, Recycling," *PBS Newshour*, http://www.pbs.org/newshour/bb/business-jan-june10-egypt_02-16/.

23. Marion Guenard, "Cairo Puts Its Faith in Ragpickers to Manage the City's Waste Problem," *The Guardian*, https://www.theguardian.com/world/2013/nov/19/cairo-ragpickers-zabaleen-egypt-recycling.

24. Kadduri, "Turning Waste into Wealth with Cairo's Garbage People."

25. Lazaro, "In Cairo's Trash City, School Teaches Reading, Recycling."

26. RT Documentary, "Zabbaleen: Trash Town," 24:48.

27. "Father Sama'an and Garbage City (Zabaleen) Part 1."

28. John Warton, Interview by Craig and Darcy Wiley.

29. Geoff Waugh, "Miracles in Garbage City, Cairo, Egypt," *Renewal Journal*, March 7, 2013, https://renewaljournal.wordpress.com/2013/03/07/miracles-in-garbage-city-cairo-egypt/.

Invitation 6: Stand Your Ground

1. Alex Philip, Interview by Craig and Darcy Wiley (Macon, France, June 2014).
2. Ibid.
3. Ibid.
4. Ibid.
5. Ibid.
6. Ibid.
7. Ibid.
8. Ibid.
9. George Otis Jr., quoted in Jack Dennison, *City Reaching: On The Road To Community Transformation* (Pasadena, CA: William Carey Library, 1999), 123.
10. Alex Philip, Interview by Craig and Darcy Wiley.
11. Ibid.
12. Ibid.
13. Ibid.
14. Ibid.
15. Iman and Lea Santoso, Interview by Craig and Darcy Wiley (Macon, France, June 2014).
16. Sumbul Ali-Karamali, "Egyptians Muslims and Christians Rising Up Together," *The Huffington Post*, http://www.huffingtonpost.com/sumbul-alikaramali/egyptian-muslims-egyptian_b_818829.html.
17. Father Sama'an, Interview by Craig and Darcy Wiley (Macon, France, June 2014).

Invitation 7: Celebrate Your Chain Reaction

1. Steve Weber, "Pride of Ukraine, Isaev's 'yes' is changing a nation," video, 5:33, https://vimeo.com/58372647.

2. Steve Weber and Anita Deyneka, Interview by Craig and Darcy Wiley (Macon, France, June 2014).

3. Weber, "Pride of Ukraine."

4. Ibid.

5. Ibid.

6. Republic Pilgrim, "Family from Charity Fund 'Pilgrim' Became 'Pride of the Country'," http://republicpilgrim.org/en/news/pilgrim/893.html.

7. Steve Weber, "Unprecented Prayer in Ukraine!," video, 3:56, https://vimeo.com/113529057.

8. Ibid.

9. Nam Soo Kim, Interview by Craig and Darcy Wiley (Geneva, Switzerland, June 2014).

10. Yoido Full Gospel Church, "Prayer Mountain," *FGTV*, http://english.fgtv.com/a5/a5_01.asp.

11. Nam Soo Kim, Interview by Craig and Darcy Wiley.

12. Ibid.

13. John Hurston, Maxine Hurston, and Karen Hurston, *Divine Desperation: 12 Powerful Insights to Help You Fulfill God's Destiny for Your Life*, https://books.google.com/books?id=Dyb8d_peXX0C&pg.

14. Nam Soo Kim, Interview by Craig and Darcy Wiley.

15. Luis Bush, "Transformation: from Poor to Blessed, A Korean Case Study," 2006.

16. Canaan Farmers School, "Canaan Farmers School Slogans," *Darrow Miller and Friends*, http://darrowmillerandfriends.com/wp-content/uploads/2013/12/ABOUT-CANAAN-YONSEI-PROGRAM.pdf.

17. Ibid.

18. Ibid.

19. Dennis Sawyers, "South Korea's New Village Movement," *The Borgen Project*, http://borgenproject.org/new-village-movement-korea/.

20. Ibid.

21. Ministry of Science and Future Planning, "Canaan Farmer School," *United Nations Development Program*, http://ssc.undp.org/content/ssc/partner/ExistingPartnerships/KFP/Projects/CanaanFarmerSchool.html.

22. "Transform World: A Starfish Structure," *Transform World*, May 1, 2015, http://www.missionfrontiers.org/issue/article/transform-world-a-starfish-structure.

Invitation 8: Lead Your Followers

1. Shiferaw Michael interview, Interview by Craig and Darcy Wiley (Macon, France, June 2014).

2. Ibid.

3. Ibid.

4. Ibid.

5. Geordon Rendle, Interview by Craig and Darcy Wiley (Macon, France, June 2014).

6. *Catechism of the Catholic Church* (n.2207), http://www.vatican.va/archive/ccc_css/archive/catechism/p3s2c2a4.htm.

7. Shiferaw W. Michael, "A Story of Hope: Children's Ministry in Ethiopian Evangelical Churches," *About Children*, http://aboutchildren.net/a-story-of-hope-children-s-ministry-in-ethiopian-evangelical-churches.html.

8. Shiferaw Michael, Interview by Craig and Darcy Wiley.

9. Ibid.

10. Ibid.

11. Ibid.

12. Dr. Dan Brewster, *Child, Church & Mission* (Colorado Springs: Compassion International, 2011), http://www.europeanea.org/wp-content/uploads/2013/09/dan_brewster_childchurchmission_revised-en-web.

13. Ibid, 116.

14. Ibid, 171.

15. Clarion Creative, "An Introduction to the 4/14 Window," video, https://vimeo.com/108187512, 0:45.

16. Nam Soo Kim, Interview by Craig and Darcy Wiley (Geneva, Switzerland, June 2014).

17. Ibid.

18. Shiferaw Michael, Interview by Craig and Darcy Wiley.

19. Clarion Creative, "An Introduction to the 4/14 Window," 1:37.

20. LaReau Anderson, ExplainED, *The Goal of Media in the 4/14 Movement*, video, https://vimeo.com/83832077.

21. Common Sense Media, *Zero to Eight: Children's Media Use in America 2013*, video, https://www.commonsensemedia.org/research/zero-to-eight-childrens-media-use-in-america-2013.

22. LaReau Anderson, "The Goal of Media in the 4/14 Movement."

23. William Damon, *Greater Expectations: Overcoming the Culture of Indulgence in Our Homes and Schools* (New York: Free Press Paperbacks, 1995), 84, 86.

24. "Be a Nurturer," *4/14 Movement*, http://www.4to14window.com/nurturer/.

25. "We Grow by Helping Others Grow," ExplainEDtv, video, 2:03, https://www.youtube.com/watch?v=2iHBW2lhwtQ.

26. Ricardo Luna, Interview by Craig and Darcy Wiley (Macon, France, June 2014).

27. Ibid.

28. Ibid.

29. John Hur, ExplainED, *My Heart for the 4/14 Window*, video, https://www.youtube.com/watch?v=dD7P45UQeqc.

30. Ibid.

31. Geordon Rendle, Interview by Craig and Darcy Wiley.

Conclusion: Choose Your Adventure

1. Elisabeth Elliot, *Shadow of the Almighty: The Life and Testament of Jim Elliot* (San Francisco: HarperSanFrancisco, 1958, 1989), 15.

2. Geordon Rendle, Interview by Craig and Darcy Wiley (Macon, France, June 2014).

3. "The Epistle of Mathetes to Diognetus," *Early Christian Writings*, www.earlychristianwritings.com/text/diognetus-roberts.html.

Acknowledgments

From Luis

Thank You my Lord and Savior Jesus Christ for knocking on my heart's door and inviting me to take up my cross and follow You to the ends of the earth. Your Great Commission has been my greatest adventure.

To Doris: you have walked with me on the journey of saying yes to God, even when that meant living in a war zone. You have exhibited the fullness of the fruit of the Spirit toward me, our children, our grandchildren, and so many citizens of the world in the regions we've visited together. I could ask for no greater partner, so full of wisdom and gentleness, than you. It has been a great joy to think back on our years of love and service in the Lord's mission as we've worked on telling our stories in this book.

To my children, Jeannine, Stephanie, Naomi, and Daniel: you have taken up the task that your mother and I have held so dear. You have served with conviction and commitment in some of the most challenging venues on this planet. And now as you serve in the daily routines of family life, I see you raising up my twenty grandchildren to be strong and courageous for the Lord.

To John Kyle, Paul McKaughan, and Derk Van Konynenburg: you have provided accountability over the decades of ministry, helping me to stay the course. To Alan and Katherine Barnhart: your support these thirty years has meant the world to Doris and me. To Milan Telian, my personal associate since the late 1980s: your loyalty, generosity, and unique perspective shaped by your successful career in government and technology have been invaluable in my life. To Wilbert Shenk, Darrell Bock, Paul Pierson, and Ron Blue: thank you for helping impact my understanding of the waves of God's mission for His global church.

To Djohan Handojo, Chairman of Transform World Connections: from your home base in Singapore, your administrative gifts empower so many to serve well wherever they are in the world. To Daniel Kim, Executive Chairman of Steering Committee of Transform World 2020: I'm blessed to have an innovative, hard-working partner in the gospel like you. To John Hur, thoughtful brother in Christ with whom I can share any burden: you were the one to first imagine a project like this, a way to share with the world the beautiful transformation that God has brought to the most challenging places. Thank you for your forward thinking and inspirational vision.

To Wess Stafford: what a privilege it has been to get to know your tender heart for the children of the world as we have worked with so many others to launch the 4/14 Window Movement. Thank you for lending your words to this project in the form of a foreword.

To Craig and Darcy Wiley who, before they ever met me, hopped on a plane to Geneva, Switzerland, to interview more than thirty agents of change in world mission: I am grateful for your sense of adventure and your insight in drawing out and putting these stories together. Darcy, thank you for your tireless work, poise, and professionalism in carrying this monumental task to completion. Craig, thank you for your expert advice in developing the proposal, finding the right publisher, negotiating the fine print, and for working with Moody Publishers to develop our title and final concept.

Thank you, Andy Stimer, friend in ministry from my time in El Salvador. Not only have you contributed greatly to the 10/40 Window Movement by crafting words and materials to communicate the cause over the years, but you have connected me with my agent, Craig, and my cowriter, Darcy, opening up a new way for these stories to be shared.

To Ingrid Beck, Kevin Emmert, Paul Santhouse, Randall Payleitner, Ashley Torres, Connor Sterchi, and the rest of the team at Moody Publishers: thank you for saying yes to this project and getting us across the finish line. I have been encouraged not only by your enthusiasm for these stories, but also by your sensitive hearts and even, at times, tears. It is a joy to partner with you to share these inspiring words with our fellow believers in the worldwide church.

To my friends Nam Soo Kim, Iman and Leah Santoso, Father Sama'an, Ezra and Anna Jin, Alex Philip, Shiferaw Michael, Raineer and Mila Chu, Corrie DeBoer, John Warton, Anita Deyneka, Steve Weber, Scott Gillis, Nabil Salib, Young Gil Lee, Ricardo Luna, Linda Grant, and Geordon Rendle:

thank you for entrusting your stories to us. May your faithful service multiply as many read these accounts and endeavor to join you in saying yes and watching God change the spiritual landscapes in front of us.

From Darcy

Thank you, Craig, my devoted friend, love, and teammate, for saying yes to expediting passports and hopping on a plane in a year full of question marks. Thank you for using your humor to turn my view around when people and prospects fell through, for solo-parenting many evenings and weekends so I could churn out these words, and for your sharp mind and creativity during editing marathons. I'm not sure how God packed so much talent and thoughtfulness into one human being, but I sure am grateful He did—and that He gave you to me.

Elliot, Farah, and Gracia, all named after that breed of people who fully trust God in adventure and adversity: you've been patient as I've closed my office door or gone away some weekends to write. We've put off some fun things. But in the midst, this book has become part of your vocabulary. It makes my heart flutter to read your journal entries of awe about God, tour the underground churches you've built in Minecraft, and watch you carry your picture Bible to read with friends on the playground.

Mom, thanks for piquing my interest in the world with your stacks of mission biographies. Thank you for always being my first reader and for getting almost as excited about my ideas as I do. Thanks, Mom and Dad, for hosting our kids when Craig and I flew to Geneva for *The Yes Effect* interviews and when we did editing marathons. Thank you, Mandy and Peter, Bobby and Leigh Ann, Jeff and Sarah, and Mom and Dad, for joining our "think-tank" on subtitles, cover design, and more. You are one creative, insightful bunch. Mama Debbie and Papa Wiley, Shannon and CJ, Sarah and Damon, and George and Jenny: thank you for the high fives via text when we passed important milestones in making this book a reality.

Julie, long-time writing partner, friend, and advocate: thanks to you and Vaughn for hosting me for a writing getaway, for always asking about my work and my inner life, and for lifting me up to the Light. To Amber and Lindsay, fellow writers and ponderers: thank you for listening and heaping on prayers and hope at harrowing moments. To Charity, thanks for your enthusiasm, generosity, and gift of connection.

Scott and Amy, teammates from a stint abroad who I now get to call neighbors: thank you for the prayer walks and for watching our kids on so many occasions, from our trip to the Detroit passport agency to the time we first met our editor. Scotia, thank you for speaking confidence into my uneasiness, for taking Gracia, and for giving me an empty house in crunch mode. Tristi, thank you for being willing to hear the good, bad, and the ugly, and to preach the gospel into my every difficulty. Via text or in person, your grace and truth always helped me recover and return to work. Mel, thank you for showing me solid ground and teaching me how to walk strong on it.

Marlene, Kristi, Jaime, Ashley, Jenny, Kathy, Michelle, Tina, Juliette, and others: thank you for praying me through sickness, accidents, losses, writer's block, computer issues, and all kinds of spiritual resistance. Thank you for the verses and blessings, the advice from those who've completed dissertations, and for the creative ways you showed you care—like rowing goals, Juliette! Thank you to the Derksens, Miles, Withams, and Wests for checking in and praying me through deadlines.

Uncle Andy, prolific writer with a missionary heart, thank you for presenting this project to Craig and me, and connecting us with your long-time friend, Luis. We admire your depth, talent, generosity, and humility, and are honored to call you family.

Luis and Doris, trailblazers in global transformation, thank you for inviting us to work with you on this beautiful book, and for facilitating communication with co-laborers from so many languages and nations along the way.

Thank you to all of the interviewees for sharing your testimonies of transformation so we, too, could come away changed. Many of you were so soft-spoken that I had to turn up the recording volume to the highest level just to barely hear your voice. God truly uses the gentle and humble to do mighty things.

Thank you to our acquisitions editor, Ingrid Beck, for seeing the potential in our proposal, for meeting us in Indy to brainstorm a fresh angle, and for letting your tears fall at the beauty of God's work in these stories. Thank you to our developmental editor, Kevin Emmert, for helping me see clearly when my eyes had crossed. Your hard work and careful attention helped make this book much more aerodynamic, keeping the power of the narratives but making them more accessible to the reader. Thank you Paul Santhouse, Randall Payleitner, Ashley Torres, Connor Sterchi, and the whole team at Moody Publishers for putting your unique vision and gifts to work for this book.

Finally, Jesus, warm light on my face, fire in my bones, kindler of possibility, thank You for being my ever-present help through all-nighters, mental overload, and every danger, toil, and snare. Thank You for stirring my longing to renew my passport and go somewhere, anywhere, well before this specific invitation dropped into my lap. Thank You for sweeping me off my feet into the adventure of *The Yes Effect*. You are the author and perfecter not only of my faith, but of this work, too (Heb. 12:2).

CHANGE IS AS SIMPLE AS OPENING THE FRONT DOOR

UNDERSTAND HIS SACRIFICE

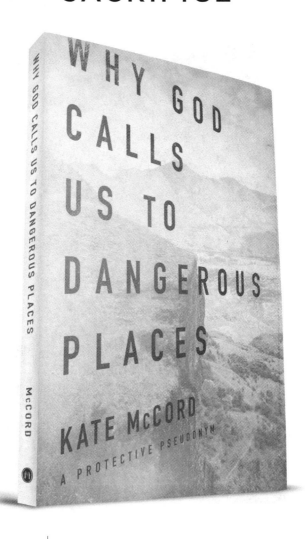

Weaving together Scripture, her story, and the testimonies of others, Kate McCord explores what is lost and gained when we follow God at any cost. Written with the weight of glory in the shadow of loss, *Why God Calls Us to Dangerous Places* leads Christians to a costly endeavor: faith.

978-0-8024-1341-3 | also available as an eBook

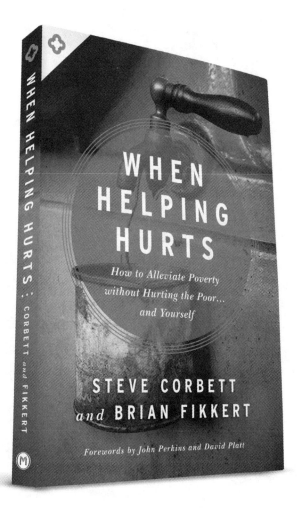

TRY SOMETHING NEW:
GIVE UP

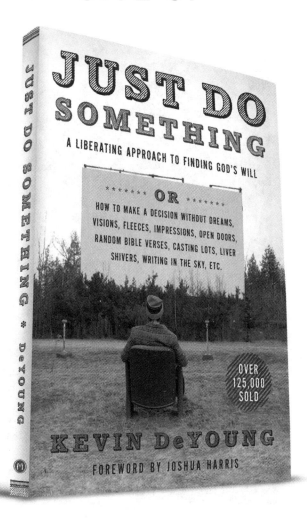